PLINY SAYS...

Pliny the Elder's Radical Take
On Healing Chronic Illness

as Told to
JOY GRAHAM

Senior Editor: Laurie Knight
Developmental Editors: Shauna Hardy and Carly Fahey-Dima
Cover Design by: Kristina Edstrom

EMPOWER
P   R   E   S   S

An Imprint for GracePoint Publishing (www.GracePointPublishing.com)

GracePoint Matrix, LLC
624 S. Cascade Ave, Suite 201, Colorado Springs, CO 80903
www.GracePointMatrix.com Email: Admin@GracePointMatrix.com
SAN # 991-6032

Library of Congress Control Number: 2023940813

ISBN: (Paperback) 978-1-955272-86-5
eISBN: 978-1-955272-87-2

Books may be purchased for educational, business, or sales promotional use.
For bulk order requests and price schedule contact:
Orders@GracePointPublishing.com

Table of Contents

Acknowledgment

One morning as I was getting ready to leave for a session with my spiritual teacher, Noa, Pliny stopped me and insisted I sit down and write. I was worried I would be late, but he was being unusually persistent, so I finally gave in. The following is what came through:

Yes, we are being very demanding this morning. And for good reason. We are wanting you to convey our salutation and benediction to your teacher, Noa. Our message is one of gratitude, that is, immense gratitude to her for having brought us together, the collective energies known as Pliny, with Dear One, the entity known in this lifetime as Joy.

We would like to acknowledge Noa for her strength of purpose as well as her physical fortitude in bringing God's message forward to you, to all of her students, and to all the cosmos. We are forever grateful.

Introduction

It was one of those crystalline moments that felt frozen and held suspended somewhere outside of time. I was making my bed, the Roomax fold-down wall bed I had purchased for my tiny studio apartment in the Potrero Hill district of San Francisco. I remember every detail of that moment, including the silky feel of the sheets and their dryer-sheet fragrance as I smoothed them on the bed. This was before I found out how toxic dryer sheets were. It was Christmastime, 2009, and as I made the bed, I had the fleeting thought *This is the last holiday season I will have before my cancer diagnosis.* The thought shocked me, but I had a visceral knowing that it was true.

After the holidays, I went to my general practitioner and asked her about a nodule under my chin that I had been aware of for several years but couldn't bring myself to investigate. It was just a little pea-sized nodule. How bad could it be?

The answer to that depends on your definition of bad. It turned out that the nodule was an enlarged lymph node caused by a type of leukemia called Chronic Lymphocytic Leukemia, or CLL. My doctors assured me that it wasn't all that bad, meaning it wouldn't kill me immediately. It was described as "indolent" and even though that means "lazy," there was no cure for it. At that time, there were no targeted immunologic therapies as there are today. But even today, the word *cure* is not applied to CLL. A person can go into remission and manage the disease, but CLL is never cured, or so says Western medicine.

From a material world perspective, my diagnosis was bad news, but from a spiritual and emotional perspective, it was a door to self-discovery and higher consciousness. And, at the risk of sounding Pollyanna-ish, I would say it was and is one of the best things that ever happened to me.

I'm not saying this from the vantage point of someone who has been cured. My disease has not been eradicated. I'm still living with it. This book is not one of those radical remission stories where the author has an unexpected, odds-defying recovery, although I do love reading those books because they give me hope and a renewed sense of possibility. This book, however, is more of a chronicle of the realizations I've had on how to live without fear, even in the face of illness and the symptoms associated with it. It's as if the Universe gifted me with a fatal disease and said, "Here ya go! We're giving you an incurable illness AND we're going to give you a long time to think about it." The gift that keeps on giving.

Since my diagnosis, and even before, I have been drawn to metaphysical ideas. I grew up in a 200-year-old house that I now believe was haunted. I was the only one in my family who seemed to notice the paranormal occurrences, so I concluded, as children will, that it was my fault. I was the crazy one. It wasn't until I was an adult looking back at my childhood that I realized the house was most likely haunted. I think that house helped me understand there is more to reality than just the physical.

The paranormal occurrences in the house, such as our upright piano playing a single note by itself and the time I felt old, withered hands over my eyes, faded over time. As I grew into adolescence, I learned to deny what I was feeling and certainly never to express those feelings. I tried to be "normal," fit in, and be liked. I was a quick learner, and there were certain rewards for that. I got good grades, went on to graduate school, married a tall, handsome man, had a career, and had a baby. In short, I was a success. But if that were true, why did I always feel so scared and insecure?

My search for solutions to my fear-based existence led me to do Werner Erhard's The est Standard Training in the early 1980s. In those days, est was in the media a lot, with many critics calling it a cult. It was a workshop-based program aimed at transforming participants' lives by showing them how programmed they were by their past and current environments. Participants were encouraged to say they "got it" when they realized the full impact of their programming. I remember thinking during one session that I had "gotten it" as the workshop leader explained that the mind is like a computer, registering and storing every incoming sensory impression and then applying the data to current circumstances. The program taught us that we were, in essence, automatons, that is, until we "got it."

My husband and I both attended basic training and afterward, evening seminars too. We were very into the whole est culture. Looking back, I see my est experience as the opening of a door— just a crack—into a new way of thinking about consciousness and relationships and self. However, the realizations I got from est weren't really compatible with the dynamics of my marriage. I remember thinking that I could either be my authentic self or I could be married, but not both. I chose to be married.

In 1982, I was initiated into Transcendental Meditation (TM) by my dear teacher, Frank Kelly, and I began a practice which I've continued to this day. I also took two levels of Reiki training in the 1990s and practiced on myself and anyone else I could get my hands on. I read every metaphysical book I could find, even though there wasn't much published in those days. (Remember, these were the days before Amazon.) I was intrigued by the Seth material channeled by Jane Roberts and loved all Ruth Montgomery's books.

Looking back, I see myself functioning on two distinctly different operating systems, one on the physical plane and one on the metaphysical with very little integration between the two. I was

x

going through the motions of my daily life, doing what was expected of me with very little understanding of how to meld the insights of my developing consciousness into my everyday world of relationships, obligations, and activities. I have now come to understand that is the work of lifetimes for most humans, that is, the integration of the human self with the pure, unadulterated soul self. I've observed that humans accomplish this task at varying rates, and some, it appears, don't attempt it at all.

I did what I thought my family and society expected of me: I went to college, earned an undergraduate degree, and then went to graduate school and earned a degree in library science, a field I had no initial interest in. It was, however, a practical choice, and besides, my mother was a librarian. It seemed like the right, and safe, thing to do. And, in many ways, it was. I always had a job, and it was pretty exciting when digital technology began to take over the field.

I was trained in medical librarianship, and for most of my forty-year library career I worked in hospital libraries. Medical librarians were among the first to go where librarians hadn't gone before, that is, into the digital world. As early as the mid-1980s, we were online with the National Library of Medicine, searching the vast medical literature database now known as PubMed. We were pioneering something important, and we knew it. As online systems became more user friendly, I began teaching end users, that is, medical professionals, how to do online searching, a skill that some librarians were reluctant to share because of the power inherent in it at the time.

Looking back, I see that I was completely indoctrinated in the Western medical model of disease-based thinking, and I totally understand how and why other medical professionals become programmed in the same way. Acceptance of the model is perhaps necessary for survival in such a stress-filled environment. So I went along with the program and never questioned its underlying

Pliny Says

assumptions. It never occurred to me to try to relate my metaphysical ideas with those of my workaday world. (That being said, I want to make it clear that I have nothing but respect and admiration for the medical clinicians, educators, and researchers who save lives every day, and who one day may save mine.)

So there I was, doggedly working full time, raising a child, taking care of my home, mostly single-handedly, when my husband of twenty-three years, out of the blue, said he wanted a divorce. What a shock! I couldn't believe he wanted out of a relationship with me. Me, the person who had tried so hard to do it all and be so perfect! I now see that in my efforts to be so perfect and to be so pleasing to others, I had completely lost touch with who I was and what I wanted. (Or perhaps I never knew who I was or what I wanted.) I had a whole lot of blankness in me that was just begging to be colored in with content, authentic content. It was a classic midlife crisis. I was forty-seven years old, and I was being forced to "re-member" myself, that is, put the Self back into myself.

After my divorce, I was more than ready to take a break from my library career and remembered that as a child I had dreamed about being a fashion designer. My favorite pastime was sketching clothes from my mother's fashion magazines. I learned how to sew in junior high school and made a lot of my own clothes as a teenager. I remember a pale pink duchesse satin gown I made for my senior prom. In my eyes, it was simple yet elegant. The prevailing poofy tulle gowns in the stores just weren't for me. But I remember my mother telling me that the fashion industry was very competitive, and that I should aim for a more refined career. I took that to mean I wasn't good enough to make it in the fashion industry. Now I realize a career in fashion was eminently suited to me and I to it, but I didn't have enough confidence and courage in those days to follow my heart.

During that post-divorce period, I was reading a book that said to "jump and the net will appear." So I jumped and moved to

Honolulu, Hawaii and enrolled in a fashion technology program at the local community college. Hawaii seemed as far away from my old life as I could get and still be in the United States. The school would teach me what I needed to know about the basics of fashion technology, even though it wasn't a famous and fancy (read: expensive) design school like the Fashion Institute of Technology (FIT) or the Fashion Institute of Design and Merchandising (FIDM). Honolulu Community College (HCC) was perfect for me and would give me a chance at the new life I was seeking.

At HCC, I learned all sorts of things, including the fact that I didn't really know how to sew and that I needed to develop a whole new level of precision and attention to detail that did not come naturally to me. I enjoyed the program, however, even though it was a lot more rigorous than I had anticipated.

Whenever a visitor came into the classroom, they assumed I was the instructor because I was old enough to be everybody's mother. I didn't care though, because I felt like one of the kids. I was enjoying materializing the ideas that I had, and it turned out I was good at it. I loved the ethnic details I was noticing in the Asian clothing people wore in Hawaii and figured out how to incorporate some of these elements into my Western-style designs. Chinese button knots and loops, asymmetrical closures, and mandarin collars all showed up in the clothing I designed as a student. They also made their way into the sleepwear line I developed later.

After graduation from HCC, I started a clothing manufacturing company called AngelWear and began designing and manufac- turing women's high-end Swiss cotton sleepwear. It was both incredibly exciting and tremendously exhausting. I worked hard at that business for over ten years and was devastated when I decided it was time to stop. I wasn't making enough money to support myself, and the financial fears were becoming overwhelming. I'm only now learning to redefine my AngelWear experience not as a failure, but as an essential and successful part of my personal growth.

It was during this time that I met Noa, who became my spiritual teacher and continues to love and guide me to this day. I expect she will continue in that role for the rest of my life. I've learned from Noa the importance of keeping an open heart and not trusting the fear-based thoughts my mind is constantly bringing to my attention. I've learned from her just how damaging those thoughts are and have figured out how to witness them, recognize them for what they are, and move on quickly.

For the past several years, I have been captivated by books on quantum physics, or I should say, the intersection of quantum science and spirituality. I don't understand any of the mathematics involved, and I'm not interested in learning, but the fact that new scientific findings are corroborating what mystics have known for centuries is terribly exciting to me.

This has been the hardest section of the book to write because I'm writing about myself and I'm on my own, telling my story in my own voice. But I know it's my job to outline how this book came to be written, and I'm happy to do it. My fondest hope is that our book may help others who are living in the fear and uncertainty that can accompany illness. Our message is this: There is a better way, and it involves shifting your consciousness. This is not to say that I think I've got it nailed. Sometimes I can shift my perspective, and sometimes I can't. I do notice, though, that over time I've become more aware of what triggers my negative thinking, and sometimes I can save myself from the downward spiral that results. I'm still learning, but *A Course in Miracles* says we teach what we need to learn. This is certainly true for me.

This book is a chronicle of the channeled conversations Pliny and I had over the course of several months. Our sessions usually took place in the morning, after my meditation and before I'd had a chance to fill the day with busy-ness. We'd discuss anything that was on my mind, and he was always happy to oblige and contribute his lighthearted take on my problem du jour. The topics were wide-ranging, mostly related to the ideas I'd gotten from my recent reading, podcast listening, or input from interactions with other people. Invariably I'd feel better after hearing what he had to say. I continue to converse with him almost daily, and I expect we will never run out of things to say.

Every day, as I cocreated this book with Pliny, I learned greater love of self, and my confidence in my own ability to heal grew, just as I hope yours does as you read it.

[Later]

From Pliny: The question of where to place the section of the book called "Tips on Reading this Book" has come up again. We are glad to have the opportunity to reconsider it because it is central to our message. We see a would-be swimmer standing at the edge of the pool, toes curled around the concrete lip, ready and wanting to plunge in but hesitating because of fears related to the temperature of the water, the depth of the pool, the presence of bacteria. Might there be stinging insects? How will their hair look when they emerge? All valid questions put forth by the thinking mind in an effort to protect the swimmer.

Our point: Timidity is not helpful here. Just dive in. Read the damn book. (We are not angry, just wanting to convey emphasis.) Read the book any way that pleases you and consider suggestions from us or any other so-called authority later, if and only if it is helpful to you.

This is why we suggest placing "Tips on Reading this Book" at the end where it may be seen as a postscript, not a prescript. The broader, deeper meaning of this issue emerges: We are not here to tell Dear One or our Dear Readers how to do things. We are here to guide them to the realization of their own innate knowing. We advocate questioning authority, internal as well as external, at every opportunity, that is, in every moment. Vive la revolution!

Chapter 1
How It All Started

I met my spiritual teacher, Noa, in the late 1990s. We were introduced by a mutual friend, and I knew immediately that she had a lot to teach me. I was ready for it. I had been in a series of abusive relationships, was unhappy in my profession, and was looking for answers. My life wasn't turning out the way I had planned. I looked like I was okay and had things together, but I felt anxious a lot of the time and was still confused about who I was and where I was going.

Noa and I started meeting regularly when neither of us was traveling. Her form of healing is a combination of talk therapy and body work. At the beginning of the session, we talk about my issues, and then I climb on the massage table and her hands intuitively go to the exact spot where healing is needed. She is able to "see" energy blockages in my body which are related to the unresolved psychological issues, either conscious or unconscious, that I've been experiencing in my life.

Sometimes it's extremely painful, but over the years, I've learned to manage the pain by letting go of my resistance to it and opening my heart, a skill which I've found useful in all sorts of circumstances. I always feel better after one of our sessions, and often, the "Noa effect," as her students call it, lasts until the next session. She is the most self-realized individual I have ever met, and I value her guidance and friendship more than anything, that is, with the exception of my connection to my own Higher Self.

I was intrigued when Noa told me there was an entity hanging out in her energy field who wanted to meet me. Noa is comfortable with spirits coming to her because they want something from her, usually healing. But this one was different. He said his name was Pliny the Elder, and he didn't want anything from her except an introduction to... guess who? Me! You can imagine my surprise; but if this Pliny person wanted to meet me, I wanted to meet him too. I had long since learned never to discount or dismiss anything Noa said, so I welcomed him like a long-lost friend, which I later found out wasn't far from the truth.

I had heard Pliny's name before and had a vague idea about who he was but had to Google him to find out specifics. He was a first century Roman author, naturalist, philosopher, and military officer. Not a lot is known about his life, except he was very close to his nephew, Pliny the Younger, and he wrote an encyclopedic work on plants and animals. He died trying to rescue a friend from the eruption of Mount Vesuvius.

As he talks about himself, note that he refers to himself in the first-person plural, "we." He later explains the reasoning for this, as he feels it more accurately reflects the composite nature of his energies in the nonphysical.

To be clear, the dialogue throughout this book is a record of the conversation between the two of us, but not a word was spoken aloud. I heard his words on an internal, mental level. The only sounds being made were of occasional snorts and flat-out guffaws from me.

[Pliny, talking about who he was historically and how we knew each other in the past.]

*In reading the Wikipedia article with you, we were struck
by the paucity of information about one as important as
Pliny. Such a shame! The personality that was Pliny was
inquisitive and adventurous. He valued discipline in all his
endeavors and was an excellent teacher. As his
consciousness developed, he became impatient with the
strictures of governments and the military, and he yearned
to be free of his official responsibilities so that he could
study, travel, and write. Does that sound like anyone you
know? It is not by chance that we have selected the
personality known as Joy to speak through. We are in
vibrational resonance, which makes communication ever so
much easier and more pleasant.*

Pliny, a friend asked me if you and I have known each other in other
lifetimes. I said that I didn't think so, but I wasn't sure.

*You are correct as usual, Dear One, we didn't know each
other on the material plane, and although we would have
loved to have said yes, you were my brother, wife, son,
what-have-you, the truth is that we have not intersected on
the physical plane at the same time in human history. Which
is not to say we haven't had plenty of influence on each
other in the quantum realm.*

I'm getting that I was a sort of cosmic advisor to you, is this correct?

*Well, that would be one way to put it. You, while in spirit,
assisted me with military reconnaissance in my duties as a
Roman Naval officer. You are familiar with the concept now
called "remote viewing," yes? For those not similarly
informed, it has been used for centuries as a military tactic
and involves the ability to receive psychic impressions of
locations and events unfolding non-locally. As you can
imagine, it gives a decided advantage to those who possess
the ability. Well, I was exceptionally skilled at this practice,
thanks in no small part to my connection to you in spirit. I*

consulted with you on all important tactical decisions. You were my strategist, and you never failed me, except maybe that one time, which we do not care to recount here in detail, but which we do not consider a failure. It was the result of a fuzzy connection between the two of us and the fact that I was tired and failed to hear your warnings.

So, you see, we are all intricately intertwined in ways unfathomable to the human mind. Kind of like a spider web, except a multidimensional web of great beauty and symmetry if it were observed from afar. And the web spells out "Some Pig!" Ah hahaha, just kidding. Oh, but we love that book called Charlotte's Web, *which is clearly not just for children. It hints at the spiritual nature of all things, a fact that children have not yet forgotten and grownups are heartened to remember.*

Your dear copy editor, the personality known as Carly, is now pointing out that some readers may be confused by our reference to a modern-day work such as Charlotte's Web. *She is asking "Did not Pliny live in the first century AD, and was not the aforementioned book written in the twentieth century?" We love the question because it affords us the opportunity to explain that from the quantum viewpoint (from which we are always coming), time is not operational, and all is known about all. We will speak more about this seeming conundrum in subsequent conversations.*

Okay, thanks for that clarification.

I marvel at how ingenious the Universe was in arranging our meeting and collaboration. I know I wouldn't have been able to hear you if you had tried to come to me directly through my own awareness. I didn't have enough confidence in my own intuitive listening to accept that there was a discarnate energy who wanted to express its ideas through me. But coming through my esteemed teacher as you did, I accepted you without question. When we first started conversing, I was amazed that you seemed to have your own voice and a distinct personality, different from mine that is. Besides that, you liked to laugh, and you liked to make me laugh too, making silly jokes and using old-fashioned terminology. And you seemed genuinely fond of me, so I didn't mind that you occasionally made jokes at my expense. It seemed like the jokes were coming from a loving and accepting place. Your wacky sense of humor was evident, right from the start.

May we remind you that we are only as wacky as our channel will allow us to be. Under other circumstances, perhaps with another channeler, we could be a great deal wackier.

Um, I think we're sufficiently wacky, but thanks!

Pliny, when our mutual friend Noa told me that you had been hanging out in her energy field just so she would introduce us, I began wondering how this would work. I took Latin in the seventh grade and liked it a lot, but I don't remember much of it now. You obviously do speak English.

You needn't worry about writing in Latin, in first century Roman style, or in any style other than your own natural voice. We will assist you in writing from that true place within yourself. Also, merely allow our voice to come through in its own true cadence, tonality, and frequency without any sort of manipulation on your part. It is best that you set up a kind of worry-free environment when you first sit down to converse with us. We say this because worry has a distinctly inhibiting effect on what is coming forth.

I am open and eager to hear you and am happy to follow your instructions. I am attempting to clear my mind of common knowledge, expert opinion, and all forms of gobbledygook. I want to write not from my own intellectual understanding of things but from the wisdom that you, Pliny, have come to impart. I'm pretty excited about this joint venture and am ready and willing to do your bidding. Just make sure you bid loud enough so I can hear you.

Ah hahaha. Don't worry, our directives will be incontrovertible, incontestable, and, moreover, so loud you can't fail to hear them. We are in complete agreement that so-called expert opinion and most certainly gobbledygook have no place in our discourse, and we appreciate your attempt to clear your thoughts of them.

We do have some tips for readers on how they might best enjoy this book, but Dear One and her book coach, Shauna, have agreed with us that it is best put at the end of the book, where it can serve more as a benediction than a restriction.

Shall we carry on?

Chapter 2
Early Conversations

The following are some of our initial conversations, which started off more formal than casual and later morphed into something more like talks between friends over coffee. Pliny's signature sense of humor never failed to put me at ease, and his down-to-earth perspective always made especially complex concepts easier for me to understand.

Our first session took place the morning of Wednesday, February 3, 2021, a few days after Noa introduced us. I was so eager to get started and very curious about what Pliny might tell me. On that morning, I sat in my comfortable Ikea lounge chair with matching ottoman, pen poised over paper on a clipboard, ready to take down every word. I decided not to use my laptop because I had heard that there was something about the kinesthetic process of writing, hand to paper, that facilitated the flow of information from the nonphysical.

I had no idea how to start, so I just dove in. To my surprise, I could hear him answer, sort of in my "mind's ear." So I asked him, "To what topic shall we apply our minds today?"

We are not taken with the idea of applying our minds. We would prefer to say "applying our consciousness" since that implies a more encompassing involvement of not only our thoughts, but also the energy from our hearts and that which resides in every cell in our bodies, not just our brains. We, of course, don't have brains or a body at the moment but are the energy of the personality who was and even today is known as Pliny the Elder. Even though we are not embodied, we possess a prodigious amount of energy. That's how we were able to come through to Noa and now, to you.

We, too, are eager to get started. Today is a new day, filled with the bright promise that only newness brings. Feel yourself enfolded by our love. We have only compassion for those of you in bodies at this time. It is not an easy time to be in a body, and we so want you to know that we are—and always have been—by your side to help in whatever way we can.

That being said, we will also say that you must be diligent and courageous in our endeavor, for we know how easily you doubt and lose interest. This work is not just for yourself, but for the ages, that is, those embodied now and generations of souls waiting and wanting to come through.

Okay, I'm prepared for a long haul, but also, it strikes me that this is a time of lightening up and pleasant co-creation with you, my new friend, Pliny!

Again, we must ask you to put distractions aside when we are working together. When we are in the flow of communication, it hinders us if your thoughts drift off, or if you reread what's been previously put down.

Okay, sorry. I value our time together and want to glean as much wisdom from you as I can. I won't reread the material until we're finished for the day. Did you want to introduce any other ideas this session?

Yes, we know you were much influenced by the book by Mark Gober called An End to Upside Down Thinking. *It introduced you to the field of quantum science and you have never been the same since. And we mean that in a good way.*

[Later that day]

I went to get *An End to Upside Down Thinking* and found that the author had written a new book, *An End to Upside Down Living,* which I bought and am now reading. Is this good?

Of course! It will add a dimension to his overall thesis; however, we feel that his first impulse was superior. You may want to reread his first title as well.

It gives me the idea that if he (Mark Gober) can do it—write a book of such profound significance—then I can do it too. I know you wrote an encyclopedic work during your lifetime, Pliny, so I am well-advised by one such as you.

Yes, that's actually why we've come to you at this time: To help you bring forth this masterpiece which is to be the crowning glory of this lifetime and many other ones and your ultimate reward for lifetimes of difficult and sometimes brutally hard work.

[The next morning]

Oftentimes it takes a warm-up period for us to effectively get through to you, so some preliminary chitchat is often helpful. Yes, you hear us now, don't you Dear One? It's about sound, resonance, and vibration and the uses of these media to induce healing. Part of the work is finding the vibratory key that unlocks your unique healing ability, and some practice is called for. We encouraged you to tone during the last part of your meditation this morning to give you some practical experience in the technique.

Yes, it felt very natural, organic, soothing, and freeing.

> *Sound healing is a topic that is well worth your further consideration. Although this modality is in its infancy, its scientific foundations are beginning to be understood and, in time, will become well-accepted as an important healing tool. In other words, sound therapy will be seen as part of the standard of care. In the future, physicians will prescribe singing rather than pharmaceuticals.*

Speaking of which, I'm really enjoying singing along to the songdance.com videos that I bought, some of which are also available free on the internet. I'm also reading Shamini Jain's book, *Healing Ourselves*, which discusses sound healing and how sound is related to consciousness and to the biofield.

> *We are glad you are open to new ways of healing. In fact, that is why we have come to you at this time. You are in the process of doing what we shall call—for want of a better word—bibliotherapy. Granted, you have always been a bibliophile, but now you are healing your consciousness and your body through the writing of a book. Its therapeutic value cannot be overstated, both for yourself and others who may read it. We shall cocreate a master work which we shall gift to the world. Our message will be read and understood by many. We will not leave you until the work is done, or, perhaps till the twelfth of never, whichever comes first.*

I appreciate that reassurance. In the past, I've read books on and experimented sporadically with what is known as automatic writing. I noticed that if I sat down to write soon after I woke up and was able to take advantage of the remnants of dream state consciousness, sometimes my handwriting would change, and the ideas would seem to be coming from someplace other than my own consciousness. But I was never really sure if I was doing it correctly, and my skepticism wouldn't allow me any lasting benefit.

You are partially correct. The benefits weren't consciously apparent to you, which doesn't mean they were without effect on the energetic level. Indeed, they were warm-up exercises to get you used to the idea of loosening your grip on content. Your mind doesn't need to create and approve what is flowing out of your pen at every instant. The metaphor of the horse and cart applies here. You need just relax in your seat and trust in the innate wisdom of that horse. He will take you home. And, you'll soon see, you'll be very glad when you get there, having greatly enjoyed the scenery along the way. We know that your personality would like immediate results; your trust is not yet built to a level where complete abandonment of the reins is possible. That is why we're undertaking these preliminary sessions. Think of them as practice sessions. You are learning to sit back and let the flow of our ideas come forth. And it may be that these practice sessions become the actual performance. At least they are recorded, so that others who might feel moved to undertake such a project have some model, some frame of reference, upon which to base their efforts.

We see that, in future times, communication with discarnate entities will be much more common. It will, in fact, become commonplace. Humanity is waking up to its true energetic nature, and there are many discarnate souls here that are coming forth to assist humans at this crucial time. Many souls currently inhabiting bodies will be hearing and benefiting from the guidance of their cosmic assistants. Some assistants will be single energetic entities, but most will be aggregate voices, such as those that present themselves to you as Pliny. We support the publication of as many of these cocreated works as possible. They will assist in the awakening of the planet, and all will benefit greatly.

Thinking about my automatic writing experiments has gotten me remembering all my other abandoned projects. I'm fearing that our book will go the way of so many of them, shelved in the closet of my workroom.

We are quite familiar with that room where your unfinished creations are stored. And what a wonderfully rich treasure trove it is! What makes you think that just because they have not been fully materialized that they are any less valuable? The fact is, they represent just a smidgen of the vast array of possible outcomes available to you. And just because they are archived on those shelves in the workroom does not mean that they're unavailable to you. You can pick one of those boxes off the shelf at any time and reanimate it. It will come to life in full, glorious color. But you had best watch what you let out of the box, for it will occupy your energies and demand you pay it the attention it's due. We are urging you to reframe your attitude about your unfinished projects only to reassure you that you needn't worry about aban- doning this book project because even if you did (which you won't), you could still at some later time revive it. We will always be here.

Okay, that is reassuring. I've also been preoccupied with the question of where and how to publish, but I hear you saying that for the moment I just need to relax and focus on content. I'm remembering how I used to approach cooking when I had my restaurant. I had no formal training in the food service industry, but I concluded that speed was more important than appreciation of the cooking process, so I trained myself to put out the most I could with the least amount of effort. Now, when I cook at home, I have to make myself slow down and remember that I'm cooking out of love for the food, for myself and the people who will be nourished by it. So, as I'm producing this book, I'm focusing on enjoying the creative process, and not worrying about how or when it will be published.

Well said. Yes, Dear One once owned a restaurant many years ago and has never fully recovered. It was very stressful for you and also taught you much about yourself and matters of business. If it pleases you, think of yourself as cooking a book right now. You have already determined the menu, but you don't have to assemble all the ingredients at this point. You don't have to decide on a font, a dedication, the front matter, the back matter... that doesn't matter, don't you see? Not a whit or even a little bit.

From our cosmic vantage point, we want you to know that what really matters is writing a book that tells the Truth as it flows from your pen through the agency known as Pliny. No lifting material from other books, scientific papers, or podcasts—as tempting as that is. Your one and only concern is listening to the whispers and occasional shouts from us and writing down what your heart tells you is true. You will be guided in technical publishing matters if you are willing to drop that sense of urgency and the inordinate need to do things "correctly." Don't make this difficult. Just let the answers come to you. "Easy does it," as they say.

Okay, I'll relax more and think of this cocreative endeavor more as an opportunity to get to know you and hang out with you and less as a project with a desired end result such as a book.

Perfect! See? We've gotten closer to a common understanding already, and we've been working together for less than a week.

Until tomorrow.

14

[The next day]

Good morning, Dear One! We know that you have been chomping at the proverbial bit to get started. We are in good disposition this morning and wondering what topics you might like to discuss today.

Whoa! I thought it was *you* telling *me* the content. I'm confused.

As you have so correctly ascertained in your journaling this morning, this is a collaboration, the rules of which we are just beginning to determine. And by "rules" we don't mean anything rigid or strict. They will be just conventions, like bidding conventions in the game of bridge. In our case, ways of conversing that will produce good results.

Okay, that sounds good. What about a question-and-answer type of format, like Neale Donald Walsch used in *Conversations with God*?

Yes, we are feeling now that might work well.

We are changing the subject here, but we feel your doubts about this collaboration arising again, like smoke from a campfire you thought you had extinguished. But now, long after you doused it, broke camp, and packed up your gear, it's smoking again. Nothing joyful or hopeful about a doused campfire. Last night it was a rip-roaring blaze. Now, just blackened coals, eggshells, and coffee grounds. It feels like cold comfort, which is not much comfort at all. That is what your fear feels like now.

Yes, that's about right.

And the only slightly comforting thing about that fear is its familiarity, like an unsavory acquaintance who's been your Facebook friend for so long you can't unfriend them now. But our job is to tell you the time is now. Time to give up the familiarity of those named and unnamed fears and choose again.

I'm ready. With you by my side, Pliny, I feel I can do anything!

[The next morning]

We must ask again that you let go of the reins. These are early days here, and we're just getting to know each other. A great opus will come through us, of that you can be sure. You knew that to be true as a child and you merely forgot it along the way. You knew that you would become a guide in service to others who had the same doubts and fears that you did. You are coming into the full expression of the personality that is Joy, and you can no longer be silent. Enough of being silent. It's time to shout it from the rooftops. Do you, perchance, have a rooftop nearby where you may shout?

Um, yes, but I think the problem might be getting up there. I can't wait to begin today's conversation, but I haven't meditated yet and wondered if there might be a better, clearer channel if I wait to open the conversation until after I've meditated. What do you think about that?

We think that you're capable of receiving our words and grasping our meanings at any time, day or night. We see the propensity of the personality that is Joy to do things by the book, according to the rules. And, we have come to tell you there is no book, and there are no rules, except those that are coming from God, and even those are being created "on the fly" so to speak. We can assure you that it's immaterial (we like that word for its literal meaning) if you communicated with us before, during, or after your morning meditation.

Now, your coffee? That's another story! Ah hahaha. A joke but not said entirely in jest. Coffee seems to be a pick-me-up for the physiology that's conducive on some days to a livelier conversation. And yes, it is an addiction. But you know that and drink it anyway. We are not berating you, Dear One.

Pliny, can you give me some tips on how to be a clearer channel for you? Sometimes I hear my own voice in your words and thoughts.

We hear you coming from a "not-good-enough" place. Please stop it at once. You are doing a beautiful job, as only you can. And again, we would remind you that this is a gradual process. It is, in fact, about the process not the end product. The process includes the following: (1) Seeing and acknowledging the truth about your thinking brain as an interpreter of sensory input not as the originator of consciousness. We like the radio analogy here. Even though the radio receiver (the brain) may be broken, the radio station continues to send out the signal (quantum consciousness). (2) Learning how to recognize and receive bodily truth and how to embody it—put it to use in everyday life. (3) Confronting the ego-created fear regarding what might happen if you learn to trust your body's input over that of the thinking brain. In other words: Learn how to live in a material world as a human but in an integrated fashion with your feet on the ground, head in the heavens.

I'm not sure if you're done with your list yet, Pliny, but this last one, number three, brings up a burning question. What is it like to have transcended the physical world and live from the place of the nonphysical?

It's nothing more or less than the end of all suffering, you see. The end of doubts, fears, pain, and all that other stuff that you think of as "bad." But we are not really talking about you transcending your body, Dear One. We are talking about realizing the true nature of the thinking brain and the role that embodied wisdom plays in creating a joyous, happy life. Hear us well: You don't have to be dead to be in heaven.

I think I love you. I'm newly in love, and that, indeed, is a heady experience.

Yes, it's the "honeymoon effect" where everything seems to be and therefore is wonderful. And it's contagious and can be perpetuated long after the honeymoon is over. Other people feel it too, not just the honeymooning couple. And it's good for all. People do their best work when they are feeling loved and adored. Just so you know, we feel that way about you. You are—you know—an aspect of us. Our scintillating lights are commingled—or entangled, to use a word now in fashion—in the quantum physics world. We feel you are losing wattage. Do you want to stop now?

I think that's a good idea for right now.

We are eternally at your service.

[The next day]

Why are we coauthoring this book, Pliny? I'm curious to get your take on it.

There have been millions of books written on the topic of overcoming illness. Many of them focus on physical aspects such as diet, exercise, sleeping well, etc. And many more have been written by those who have overcome their illnesses by spiritual and emotional means. Most of these books are prescriptive in that they say, "Do it the way that I did it and you may recover as I did." We are presenting an alternative approach that is more descriptive rather than prescriptive in nature. We are, in conversational format, laying out the dialogues that we, the entity known as Pliny the Elder, are having with Dear One as she expands her consciousness. We are expressing our wisdom through her unique creative lens. We are describing the sometimes joyful, sometimes painful experiences that she is processing.

18

> *This is as much about the healing of Dear One as it is about service to humankind. Our fondest hope is that both she and our Dear Readers will benefit from this work we are undertaking together.*

I have another question: Who do you think will read this book? Someone, I hope. I woke up thinking that it deals mainly with my own personal stuff and that it won't be of interest to the general population.

> *You are absolutely correct in the latter part of your assessment. It will be deemed absolute rubbish by 95 percent of the population. Nay, 99 percent. Does that matter? Not a whit or even a little bit. Your concern is to write it as it comes to you through us. And the fact that it is very personal is the precise reason that it will be so infinitely valuable to the remaining 1 percent. That is the sole reason for all this work, which is not really work but more like play. Child's play.*

Pliny, ever since I met you and we started conversing, I've been worried about how to best organize this book. I'm concerned that since the topics of our daily talks do not have a logical sequence, a book arranged chronologically will be unappealing to our Dear Readers.

> *Yes, we have noted your continued anxiety about this topic, and we have tried to reassure you that all will be well. Your anxiety stems from the basic problem that we are speaking different languages. We are expressing our ideas in "God Speak" language while Dear One's native language is "Ego Speak." That does sound somewhat harsh, doesn't it? And we do not intend it in a mean-spirited way at all. We are merely describing the ego-based language she learned from infancy, which was reinforced by parents and teachers and which she has been using ever since to convey ideas to others. It is the language learned and used by every human,*

unless they are gifted poets or graced with the great good fortune of a spiritual awakening of some flavor, such as the one experienced by Dear One in meeting the collective entity known as Pliny. We are, in essence, a GSSL (God Speak as a Second Language) teacher. In this case, we are reintroducing the student to the language she knew at birth but forgot.

Does that mean that all of what you're calling Ego Speak language is inherently false?

Yes, but some ego-based writings are more untrue than others. In our experience, it depends on the degree to which the ego has taken concepts and corrupted them for its own purposes. Yes, even some of your own writings are in that corrupted category, including those on seemingly divinely inspired topics such as self-love and self-esteem. On the surface, this material seems benign, but to the extent that it has been usurped by the thinking mind, it is virtually useless. That is why we are attempting to bypass your thinking mind when we send forth ideas. We're hoping that they remain untainted and uninterpreted by that busy, busy mind of yours. We have been, so far, mostly successful in this endeavor. Whenever you find yourself hesitating with wording or perhaps correcting our cadence, please stop and consider where the ideas are coming from. And we know that Shauna, your dear book coach, can easily distinguish genuine God Speak from gobbledygook. That should be reassuring.

Yes, thank you for that reassurance, I think.

Learning a new language is generally not easy for adults, and the situation is made even more difficult by the fact that Dear One has a tiny bit of conceit regarding her Ego Speak language skills and, at times, tries to override our expressions with her own. There is much remedial work to be done;

and here again, we are not blaming, merely observing. We are gratified to note, however, that Dear One is an extremely dedicated and highly motivated learner, perhaps because of the "incurable" label that has been applied to her current bodily condition. For whatever reason, we feel that her God Speak language skills are coming along nicely.

I'm sorry, but I'm still really confused about the best way to organize this book.

We feel your unease, Dear One. This seeming conundrum serves as an excellent teaching tool, for it can be generalized to circumstances other than just organizing content. The larger question is this: How to function effectively, happily, and lovingly with oneself and one's fellow travelers in the often-ambiguous material world, whilst maintaining connection to the divine and to Heaven, your real home.

Here, we must remind you that in Truth, there is no dilemma, no paradox, no conundrum even. You are, and always have been, first, foremost, and forever, a child of God. Nothing could ever or will ever invalidate that. The seeming problem begins to arise the moment you come down the chute, also called the birth canal, and arrive in a body. That is the moment you begin to forget who you are. Yes, it seems like a cruel setup, but it is not. It is merely the most effective way for souls to advance in their development. It is, you see, the way the human learns to return to Self and her godlike nature. It is through the trial and error of experience, and, infrequently, direct revelation, that the soul grows through its time on Earth.

Dear One is tugging on the reins, wanting to get back to the original question, which we have now totally forgotten. Ah hahaha! Just kidding. The question at hand is the organization of the book. Dear One and I seem to have reached an impasse. But an impasse is impossible in the quantum.

We like the sound (but not the idea) of impossible impasses. It reminds Dear One of the dead-end city streets she has encountered in France. They are called impasses. The street name lets you know right up front that there is no outlet on the other side. Very kind of those naming the streets, we would say. Saves a lot of walking.

But we digress. Here is our inclusive, quantum-style resolution to this conundrum which never was a conundrum in the first place: Dear One will continue to take dictation, and we will present ideas in perhaps a more organized, thematic way, after which she, with her exceptional organizational skills, will wrestle those ideas into straitjackets according to chapter headings. Ah hahaha. No, just kidding. Straitjackets have a negative connotation, so we will forthwith abandon that metaphor and search for one that will more accurately describe this brilliantly organized cocreation.

BING! She's received it, a visual image of the old-fashioned card catalog that Dear One knew from her early days as a librarian. She is picturing the great arched hallway of the Free Library of Philadelphia, where Dear One got her start as a rookie librarian. Yards of card catalog drawers lined that hallway, and librarians wore headsets to answer the constant phone calls from the public inquiring about the holdings of the mammoth Free Library of Philadelphia, or FLoP, as it was (and maybe still is) affectionately called by its familiars. She is recalling that the librarians did not wear roller skates, although we think that would have been a nice touch. In the drawers of the catalog were 3x5 inch cards filed alphabetically by main entry—either author, title, or subject.

Our magnum opus will be arranged conceptually as a card catalog, but with only subject cards. We won't need those author and title cards. Now, Dear One urgently needs to know whether the subject chapter headings must be arranged alphabetically, and we can only sigh and breathe deeply and say, "As you wish". Yes, we have infinite patience and love for you.

(Earlier, as part of my relentless anxiety about how to organize the book, Pliny had suggested another organizational metaphor, a meal of tapas.)

We have noted your tendency to worry about what comes after the transcription process, and we can only reassure you that the way will be made clear. Stop worrying about the final form of the book and put one foot in front of the other. The organization of the book will come to you during periods of meditation or relaxed introspection. It will not appear as a banquet spread out on long tables but as a series of small plates, made available when you are ready to consume them. Think of this joyous process as a meal of tapas, akin to the one Dear One experienced in San Sebastian, Spain. In this case, the presentation of each exquisite plate will take place over days, not hours. One day, an appetizer will be brought to you. Several days hence, a side dish will appear, and so forth until all the courses have been consumed, and we will experience the luxury of complete satiety. We will be filled, but not overstuffed, with wholesome, flavorful, nutritious food. Now, doesn't that metaphor appeal more than the drudgery you were calling forth previously?

Yes. But now, I'm fretting over what content to include in the book. It has become a herculean task, akin to mucking out the Augean stable to organize it all.

An unfortunate metaphor, Dear One. The content of our conversations is not akin to muck in the least! Ah hahaha!

Sorry, that wasn't what I meant.

Here's a thought that will ease your mind: There is no shortage of Pliny material in the cosmos. We are like a cosmic electrical outlet that you can plug into at will. (Please insert a drawing of electrical outlet here.) There is no shortage or scarcity of electrical current there, right? No, or hardly ever we should add. Sometimes the electrical device that's connected to the power source malfunctions, but rarely is there an interruption in the current.

Dear One is now remembering a time when the current went out at her house due to a blown transformer at a local substation. That is what she was told. Her whole neighborhood had no electrical power, to which we can only reply: We have never, nor will we ever, blow a transformer because we are not powered by transformers. You can take that to the bank. The Pliny energy does not break down, just as the energy that is Dear One has and will be forever perpetuated, into perpetuity. And that's a long, long time [Pliny humming "The Twelfth of Never" melody].

The point we were attempting to illustrate with the electrical outlet image is this: Since there is no shortage of Pliny energy, there never will be a shortage of Pliny content for the book, so you needn't worry about incorporating all the previous conversations into the organization of this book.

Yes, yes, we know. What we've previously put forth is some really good stuff. Important stuff. But there's plenty more good stuff where that previous good stuff came from. Better, even, because we're just preparing the channel. The radio is getting nice and warm, and those old-fashioned vacuum tubes are glowing with a radiant, healing light. You're getting the idea now, aren't you, Dear One?

We are now humming the Carole King song, "You've got a Friend" That's all ya gotta do, Dear One, just call our name.

Joy Graham

[Later]

The question of whether to include drawings in the text has come up. As he dictates, Pliny has been designating insertion points for drawings with the directive for me to do simple, pencil drawings to illustrate the metaphors he is discussing. I had been mentally preparing to do that when my book coach informed me that the inclusion of drawings would add to the final cost of the book for buyers. She suggested I ask Pliny about it, and the following is his response:

In the excitement of all this book-writing fervor, we feel that Dear One has lost sight of a few basic principles. Allow us to remind her. The Pliny energies are here in service not just to her, but to all humankind. Our mission is sacred and cannot be tainted by material world considerations. An example of this is the question of whether to include drawings in the text. Her book coach tells her that drawings would add to the final cost of the book, that is, make it more expensive for potential buyers, possibly resulting in fewer books sold. And she has come to us to ask our (Pliny's) opinion on whether we should, indeed, include drawings.

We would respectfully and gently respond that we are not in the least concerned about the number of books sold. In the cosmic, non-linear world, there is no order of magnitude, that is, bigger does not equal better. More books sold does not equal a better outcome. We have said before that if one person buys the book and benefits from it, we are delirious with happiness. Actually, we are already delirious with happiness because Dear One here has already benefited greatly from writing it.

We are creating a master work together, an example of cocreativity in its highest and best form. It will illustrate to our Dear Readers how effortless and rewarding it is to cocreate with discarnate energies. By allowing us to speak through her pen (and pencil) she is thus encouraging them to do the same using the same or different media.

Many books such as ours will be called into creation, and through the mediation of a myriad of human souls, much will be revealed about the mysteries of the Universe. What was previously known only to sages and mystics will become available to the proverbial man on the street. Humanity is now on a crash course with annihilation, and although we do not wish to dwell on this potentially disastrous outcome, the magnitude of the danger is becoming increasingly apparent for all on planet Earth to see. Humankind must change course, and can change course, with assistance from those of us in the quantum realm who have come forth as guides and assistants to steer humans to a healthier future.

Another reason for this cocreative endeavor is to showcase the many talents of Dear One. Nay, nay, enough of your naysaying. Do not forget that you, Dear One, are nothing more or less than a fractal of the holographic Universe. To deny your own talents is to deny those of the collective. In you are all things and beings, and in all things and beings are you. Dear One loves drawing, and her drawings will add a leavening effect on this somewhat dense treatise. They will add a note of playfulness. Her obviously non-professional renderings will add greatly to the overall whimsical tone of the book.

Pliny, a solution to the issue of the drawings came to me recently. Rather than me doing actual drawings why not ask our readers to visualize them using their own prodigious imaginations? It will be cocreative and fun for everyone.

We like it. No, we LOVE it! It will be up to our Dear Readers, then, to search for and insert images from their own personal mental image galleries when drawings are called for in the text. Brilliant!

[Later]

I'm going over some of our past conversations and need to ask this important question: How do you feel about your words being edited?

Good, but we are at a loss to understand how our words could be improved upon.

Well, sometimes I think of a better way to say something, but I'm not sure if it's your voice that's talking or if it's my own voice. I'm asking because some entities give instructions to their channelers that the words of their transmissions must not be tampered with in any way.

We agree that willy-nilly tampering with our content is not a good idea, but we judge you to not be a willy-nilly tamperer. We did notice that several times you changed our words as you typed the content from the original handwritten sheet, and we wanted to assure you that this is perfectly permissible and right to do with only one word of warning. Please be well attuned to our frequency, and we will let you know in no uncertain terms if you begin to edit something that is beyond your limited range of knowledge and thus create misleading content. That is why it is so essential to be working closely together, so that we stay finely tuned into each other's frequency and avoid any potential misleading statements or, God forbid, gobbledygook.

I'll be listening intently.

Here's another tip you might find helpful. When you are in the process of selecting content for this masterpiece or editing what has already been set down, we want you to stop and ask yourself, "Is Pliny here, and does he have his hand on the throttle?" We would liken our book project to a jumbo jet, or, perhaps in our case, a two-seater Cessna. In either case, both pilot and copilot must have their hands on the throttle, FAA regulations. And my sign to you, when you are in doubt as to content, is that you will feel our collective hand on yours to indicate our approval. Yes, that tingly feeling you just got in your right hand. That will be our indicator to you that we are with you in the cockpit, and all is, indeed, well.

Chapter 3
What's Quantum Physics Got to Do with It?

As I was transcribing the conversations from handwritten to digital format, I noticed a lot of the material was based on ideas that I recognized from my readings about quantum physics. I can't remember exactly where or when my interest in this subject began, but I do remember that it impacted me greatly, like the proverbial ton of bricks. I started with Mark Gober's *An End to Upside Down Thinking* and after that, began reading every book and listening to every podcast on the subject I could find. I was especially interested in material on the intersection of quantum science and spirituality or consciousness.

Some of the material was over my head, requiring a knowledge of physics and mathematics, and included ideas about black holes and string theory, all of which are baffling to me. But I found I could grasp the more philosophical ideas and, man, was I hooked! I remember talking to a friend about my discoveries and exclaiming, "This changes everything!" which, of course, it does, and in a very good way, too. I was like a born-again Christian, a convert to a new religion, and in my eagerness, I was spreading the good news to anyone who would listen. Fortunately, I am blessed with friends who are open and even eager to listen to what I have to say, and several became converts like me.

I'm using the terms *quantum science, quantum physics*, and *quantum mechanics* interchangeably, which is probably terribly incorrect. Frankly, I don't think it matters that much, and I think Pliny would agree. I say this because Pliny doesn't think much of anything matters except love, joy, happiness, laughter, etc. He's definitely not interested in overthinking things, or thinking at all, really.

In an effort to make this section on quantum physics easier to read and understand, I've decided to add subject headings, an idea Pliny suggested earlier using the image of an old-fashioned library card catalog with subject heading cards.

Particles and Waves

One of the tenets of quantum science is that photons (small bits of light) can express themselves either as waves or particles. The famous slit-screen experiment of the 1920s demonstrated that whether the photon showed up as a waveform or a particle depended on whether it was being measured or observed. Waveforms indicate possibilities whereas particles represent the collapse of the wave into a particle of matter. My interpretation of this is that once I've observed the possible outcomes in a situation and chosen a course of action, or formed an opinion, the wave of possibility collapses and matter is created.

Here's how our particle/wave conversation went:

I have the feeling you have something to impart. Is it important?

> *Everything we impart is important. Don't you agree? And every tidbit is every bit as important as every other tidbit. By the way, there is nothing tiny about our tidbits, when, in fact, even the smallest detail down to the most minute particle is worthy of your undivided attention and consider-*

ation. We are bringing this up because we would like you to understand this in a very personal way. The precious little photon shows you that you don't have to choose to be one thing OR the other. You can be one thing AND another at the same time. And why not be both? No need to choose, until, of course, it's prudent to do so.

Pam Grout, one of my favorite authors, calls the quantum realm the "FP," which stands for the "field of potentiality," where infinite possibilities are at play. In other words, those little packets of light (photons) are expressing not as molecules which make up solid matter, but as waves, which include a dizzying array of possibilities. In her books, *E-Squared* and *E-Cubed*, she asserts that to work with the quantum realm, you really have to believe very deeply that the Universe is a bountiful place where it's safe to be you. She outlines a number of thought experiments that confirm the beneficence of the Universe and validate the hypothesis that consciousness creates matter.

One such experiment had a huge impact on me during a time when I was on vacation in Nice, France. I was by myself, and I had come down with bronchitis and was really needing some confirmation that all was, indeed, okay. When I had recovered enough strength, I did one of Pam's manifestation experiments and the results blew me away.

Following her directions, I chose an image, a butterfly, with the idea of manifesting in some form at least one butterfly that day. I was staying in the middle of Nice, a large town, so the likelihood of seeing a butterfly seemed remote, but I was going to try. After a long day of shopping and sightseeing I still had not seen a single butterfly and was about to give up. But wait! There, on the cellphone case of a woman seated opposite me on the bus going home, was a jewel-encrusted butterfly! "What a powerful manifester am I," my ego crowed, wanting to take credit, as egos do. The real credit, of course, belongs to quantum consciousness, the generator of all things miraculous. And I, as Pliny tells me, am but one fractal of its magnificence.

Encouraged by my success, I repeated the experiment the next day using a different image, a yellow truck. I wound up seeing yellow trucks all over the place, but mainly because French postal service vans are all yellow. No matter, I still counted the experiment as a success.

We remember how profoundly you were affected by those experiments. At the moment, however, we ascertain that you are feeling very particle-y. That is, you're feeling dense, like matter, although you do know that at any moment you can go into your wave-like form merely by parking your thinking mind outside the door and entering into the expanded quantum state. Sit down, crank up your binaural beats, and up, up, and away you go! No need to think when you're in this expansive state. Thinking merely gets in the way and leads you astray at every turn.

Brains, Thoughts, Mind, and Consciousness

I'm a little confused, or I should say a lot confused, about how my brain relates to my thoughts. Also, how does my mind relate to my brain and my consciousness?

Good questions, all. And we are glad you're confused, because it's been said by very learned quantum scientists that if you think you understand quantum physics, you obviously don't. The human mind, which we will define momentarily, isn't wired to logically understand quantum principles, hence our propensity to describe quantum effects in terms of felt experiences, which are easily understood by humans. Most quantum physicists prefer to describe quantum ideas using mathematics, although that makes it difficult, nay, impossible, for you to comprehend.

The terms brain, thoughts, mind, and consciousness are all interrelated. But in giving them different names, humans have made them into separate things, each requiring its own definition. Language does that to otherwise perfectly content and unified concepts. (Sigh.) Such a shame, but humans aren't yet fully aware of their ability to communicate telepathically, hence the need to use language and in so doing, naming them and thus making them seem separate.

Carly, our esteemed copy editor, is calling for some clarification on the previous paragraph. She is describing it as complex and is suggesting a rewording so it can be more easily understood by our reader. We are in whole-hearted agreement with Carly. The idea of everyday human consciousness is, without doubt, the most difficult concept for humans to grasp, primarily because they can't get outside their consciousness box to give it a good look-see. A good look-see is available to humans only via the quantum, something we will explore in more detail in subsequent conversations.

The point we were endeavoring to make, however, is not about the complex nature of consciousness, but rather, the limitation that language places on humans in their search for Truth. We are not denying the usefulness of language in human affairs. We are merely pointing out that language can promote the erroneous perception of separation. You know, those problematic personal pronouns such as me, you, he, she, and they. We could go on, but we won't.

Okay, I get it, but to make it easier to communicate via language with you and our Dear Readers, may I suggest some definitions for each of the above concepts, based on my readings? Otherwise, things may get muddled.

Yes, we certainly don't want "things" to get any more muddled than they already are!

Can we agree that the brain is the organ that's located (anatomically speaking) in the human head? It receives and registers signals from the environment. According to what I've read, there is now scientific consensus among forward-thinking physicists that the brain is *not* the source of those signals, nor does it create thoughts and emotions; rather, thoughts and emotions are created by consciousness and are then received and registered in the brain. The primacy of consciousness theory, as articulated by quantum physicist Peter Russell, holds that consciousness is more funda-mental than matter. I take that to mean that consciousness gives rise to matter rather than matter creating consciousness, as Newtonian physics taught. What do you say about this, Pliny?

I wouldn't spend too much time on that line of thinking. It is merely what's so, always has been, and always will be. Your creative power lies in your consciousness. It is the basis of what you are calling the law of attraction, although we do feel that much of what is written about the law of attraction is a bunch of gobbledygook. And you know how we feel about gobbledygook!

No, wait. I want to talk about this! I was thinking about this because I was anticipating feeling unwell tomorrow because I'm getting my second COVID-19 vaccine dose and having to deal with the contractor being here all day and then the effort of having to go to quartet practice. I play in a string quartet and love the music and the other musicians, but it takes a lot of energy to show up at the weekly rehearsals and play the difficult music, which is made even more difficult because I am my own worst critic. Because of all that, I sometimes see quartet practice as an obligation rather than fun. Dealing with obligations is one of my weak points, and I see that if I anticipate a hard time, it's almost as good as done. That is, I've created what I don't want by my picturing and anticipation of discomfort.

The Puppy Poo Principle

We are not prone to dispensing dictums, but here's a really good one for you to know and remember: Envision only what you want, not what you don't want. Once you realize that your reality is generated by your consciousness, you will be well-advised to keep a tight leash on that puppy. He will want to chase after butterflies and trip you up by running in front of you, but for his own safety and yours, you must always be in control, keeping him close to you, on your left side preferably. Another task would be to house-break the puppy. You must be ever vigilant for signs that he needs to go outside. Be proactive by preemptively taking him out on a schedule. What we are really suggesting is that you be very watchful of your feelings and moods. Investigate how a downturn in affect might be related to the picturing of something you don't want. We will call this the "Puppy Poo Principle."

Yes, delightful! Now whenever I envision something I don't want, I'll picture my puppy pooping in the house.

Illness and Responsibility

Excellent! We know that Dear One is an expert at connecting dots, but we will just include this next profound pronouncement for added emphasis. Since consciousness creates the conditions from which matter arises on the local level, your consciousness, including what is called the subconscious, has created all the lovely manifestations of your illness. We are describing them as lovely because they are proof positive of the power of your consciousness to create matter. Think of them as testimonials to your ability as a creator and love them for that reason too. You are responsible for creating them; therefore, you will be able to respond to them and, in fact, allow them to disappear, if you so choose.

Totally understood and accepted, especially since I know that there is no shame or blame involved in this definition of responsibility.

We are glad you are wise enough not to blame yourself for your illness. There is certainly no cheese down that part of the maze, to use an analogy from Dear One's est training.

Ah! We are pleased to see a question has just come in from your book coach, the personality known as Shauna. She has asked: "If we've created illness, why aren't we able to easily remove it? And how are we able to look upon illness and other unfortunate events in our lives without feeling shame or falling into victim mode?"

We love this type of collaborative discussion and would encourage her to ask more questions should they arise. Let us address the first question. And to that we would say, illness comes upon humans neither quickly nor easily. Illness is related to misguided thoughts over a period of time, which are correlated with unhealthy thought fields. This leads to perturbations in the organism's energy field and manifests as less than optimal energy flow within the organism's energetic channels. It is a process that does not generally happen overnight. Why, then, would one expect the illness to be easily removed as Shauna is suggesting?

Although instantaneous healings have been documented and occur more frequently than one might expect, that is not the norm. Normally a disease is resolved one molecule at a time, as the organism corrects its faulty thought forms and healthy energy flow is restored. This is a crucial concept to understand, especially for those who are assessing the progress of their healing by measuring their symptoms. Oftentimes, healing may be taking place on an energetic level while not manifesting on a physical level until a period of time has passed. Humans may get discouraged in their attempts to heal and say, "Oh, this isn't working," and give up trying. This is why it is important not to let the persistence of physical symptoms determine your frame of mind. In fact, it is that very thing—your expanded, hopeful, loving, frame of mind—that is the most influential factor in your healing.

Shauna also asks how one may avoid feeling shame about unfortunate events in one's life or the existence of disease in the body. We would remind her that many an enlightened being has come down with rheumatism, gout, and yes, hemorrhoids. Many fine people get sick and some even die of their diseases. Illness is not an indicator of one's degree of spiritual development. It is merely an indicator that one is human. One does not want to feel ashamed about being human, does one? NO, one does not. Especially since being a fully functioning human is your one and only job here on the planet. And neither guilt nor shame are helpful in that endeavor.

The Unhealed Healer

Thank you, Pliny, for addressing Shauna's questions. Another variation on this theme came up the other day when my teacher, Noa, said that I was an "unhealed healer." So, I opened up my tattered volume of *A Course in Miracles,* another source of truth and inspiration to me, to read its definition. It says that unhealed healers have not yet accepted the idea that the body does not create illness even though they may be endeavoring to help others who come to them for healing. It gives examples of theologians and psychotherapists who are treating people but still put faith in the physical, that is, in the constructs of the egoic mind. I guess I'm proud of the fact that I have a deeper understanding than that, and I've pretty much accepted the primacy of consciousness notion that quantum physicists are suggesting. So, I'm wondering, if I'm so onboard with these ideas, why am I not yet healed?

Ah, the reprise of Dear One's familiar theme song. It's called "If I'm So Smart, Why ain't I Healed?" Firstly, we would say with much love and respect, "Yes, you are smart, for a human." Ah hahaha! Secondly, we would assure you that you are, in Truth, healed. You have heard the Truth behind many ideas and have embraced it enthusiastically. Here we are using the word enthusiasm deliberately for its original Greek derivation (en theos, or in God). And yes, we are acknowledging, albeit grudgingly, that those Greeks did have a few good points, inspired language being one.

Trust and Healing

You are assuming that since your symptoms do not appear to be subsiding that you are not healed, and this is the crux of the seeming dilemma. You want your symptoms to resolve, and you want them to do it on your timetable. Is that not so? And can you sniff out just a whiff of egoic thinking in that? Sort of like a lingering fart? Ah hahaha. We don't mean to be offensive, and we can feel that Dear One is slightly put off by our vulgarity.

Here's another way of looking at this ego-driven dilemma: What if you were so relaxed, so expanded, and so in love with yourself and everybody and everything that you could merely lie back and float effortlessly in the warm waters of Lake Gratitude, trusting that you will be held afloat by the laws of a benevolent Universe? There is where the healing of your symptoms lies.

You know you understand and accept many of the ideas behind quantum physics, that is, as science knows them today. So now that you know, and you know that you know, and we know that you know, and you know that we know that you know, the time now is to just DROP IT! Yes, we are shouting. Just drop all the cerebral stuff and lie back in trust and gratitude. Trust in God, which is something often said by humans but very rarely done because few really understand what's entailed in the process of trusting. It involves giving up all the mental constructs you've put in place over the years to keep you safe. But we know, don't we Dear One, your cerebrum is not where your safety lies.

Going forward, you will be spending more and more time at Lake Gratitude, relaxing, swimming, chatting with friends, enjoying life. While there, you will be receiving continuous instruction and inspiration from us and the voice of God. We will be assisting you in your dreams and in your every waking nanosecond. If by some unfortunate turn of events, you find yourself in some location other than Lake Gratitude, you can zip back there by merely speaking our name, either out loud, whispered, or just silently. All will work equally well. We see that you have run out of paper, so we will be stopping here for today.

The Evolution of Quantum Consciousness

Can we get back to the subject of quantum physics now?

In truth, we have never strayed from the topic of quantum physics because it is a subject that encompasses everything, a sort of "theory of everything," even though mainstream science has not corroborated this truth at the time of this writing. The field of quantum physics is only one hundred years old, a mere nanosecond on the human timeline, but it is advancing rapidly in its ability to accurately describe the nature of the Universe. The reason for this rapid advancement in understanding is that in recent years there has been a cosmic restructuring of the "All That Is," which includes a restructuring of the human energy field. This is what is making it possible for humans to make these leaps in their understanding of what you are calling quantum conscious-ness. Previously, the human nervous system could not manage such feats.

I've been reading Suzanne Giesemann's book, *Wolf's Message.* She is a medium who uses evidence in the physical world to validate the messages she is receiving from the spirit world. She has received information confirming that the Universe and everything in it is now in a period of realignment, and that our solar system is realigning with the heart of the galaxy and individuals are realigning to their own hearts.

We are amused. Dear One is always happy to find information that confirms her own conclusions. She looks for validation from outside herself, not yet fully under-standing how to access that information from within. We are helping her with this basic developmental step of becoming self-referent. We like this word not only because it sounds a bit like "self-reverent," but also because it harkens back to her days as a reference librarian. One of the important librarian rules was never to give information "off the top of your head," accurate though it may be. No, the answer had to be found in an authoritative published source. So, Dear One learned early on that her own knowledge was not worth much, that she needed to refer to sources of information more authoritative than her own. And perhaps it was a good rule for reference librarians in those days. We hate to think of all the spurious information those salacious librarians might have put out had it not been in place. But in the context of her own life and developing her own cosmology, is this rule still valid? Is it useful? We think not, on either count.

The Torus

I'll keep that in mind. Thank you. Speaking of librarianship, you know I read all the time, right? Well, in my reading lately I've been coming across the word *torus* more often than might happen by chance. Interesting, huh? A torus is a donut-like geometric shape that describes the energy flow in all things, from the micro to the macro.

You find it merely "interesting" that this word has come to your attention multiple times during the past few months? We have been standing on our collective head trying to draw your attention to this concept because it has something significant to teach you.

A torus is a structure that describes the dynamic energy state of All That Is. Yes, it does slightly resemble a donut. (Can we please insert an image of a torus here, lest our Dear Readers be thinking about Krispy Kremes? We all know how distracting they can be.)

It can be very useful to hold the image of a torus in your awareness during meditation because its structure represents the flow of consciousness both on the physical plane and in the quantum realm. It is the structure of that nonphysical thing that physicists refer to as the field of potentiality, and mystics call God. This is new news here, by the way, and not generally known in the material world, so please stop trying to validate it with your thinking brain or, God forbid, by Googling it.

Shauna is asking us to expand upon our previous audacious pronouncement linking the torus to God. We are happy to oblige. We are amazed and delighted at the variety of God concepts and images that humans hold, and, if Dear One is representative of other humans, their ideas about God are constantly changing. Of course, we are not about to tell anyone that their concept of God is false, but here is an additional idea worth considering. Why not consider God to be the same bioenergetic pattern that has been shown to make up every human, the torus? We cite the "As above, so below" dictum as well as the biblical verse "So God created man in his own image" in support of this proposition. Would it not make sense for the creator to have the same form as the creation? The part we like best about this concept is that the heart is at the inside center of the human torus form, the location of the physical heart in the human body. We like the symbology of this because it affirms the centrality of love, as represented by the heart, in the Universe.

Thank you, Pliny. I like the idea myself, but I was wondering how this news will be received and was even anticipating some rebukes in the form of snide emails from experts.

Remember what is said about the proof in the pudding? In her most recent meditation, Dear One tried out the torus image and found it delicious, better even than Krispy Kremes, she thinks. During this meditation, she was picturing the torus and then put her hands on her heart. She felt what she calls a "buzzy expansion" of her awareness and a "blooming" in her heart area. She also experienced feelings of optimism, safety, and trust. Is this not proof positive of the power of the torus? We rest our case.

To conclude our discussion on this topic, we would like to acknowledge that this recent restructuring of consciousness is what is enabling us to come through to you now. Your new heart-centered alignment makes it possible for you to hear our collective voice. We are just the tip of the iceberg, the first of the pioneers in covered wagons who will be converging on the edge of the wilderness—that ragged edge of the collective human awareness—ready to venture into the new reality. There will be many more voices like ours on the westward journey. Please know that we are honored to play this role in assisting humans in the development of their consciousness.

We would also add that Dear One's personal awakening is coming along nicely, and although we do not foresee any sudden light-bulb moment for her, we note in her a gradual easing into truth and a slow-but-steady easing off of all that is not truth, such as the lies that she used to tell herself constantly. She is now recognizing lies as lies. We call that progress, and we are happy to be part of it.

Unity Consciousness

Please say more about how ideas from quantum science can be applied to everyday living.

One important idea involves the realization of the unity of all consciousness. It is central to what seems unfathomable from your point of view—but really is not—if you stop trying to use your mind to understand. In your world of physicality, people and things seem to be so separate and, yes, distant from each other. Although we totally understand how and why people come to this conclusion, it is not helpful if one wants to understand one's true nature and the true nature of the Universe.

The true nature of the Universe is all-inclusive. It's a "both/and" realm where we see that all possibilities exist. We see you scanning your storehouse of accumulated knowledge to try to come up with pertinent content and we truly wish you would not do that. You must trust us enough to let us drive the cart. Try to put aside your worry that we may be going toward the ditch. And yes, when we first sit down to talk, it may seem as though we're meandering a bit; that is truly okay. Not only is it okay, but it's also absolutely necessary to warm up the channel of communication at the beginning of a session. We assure you that our connection is strong enough to survive over time. I will not leave you, abandon you, mid-stream.

Speaking of the evolution of human consciousness, I'm encouraged by recent scientific breakthroughs showing that the human brain is more flexible and capable of change than had been previously thought. Through consistent and diligent effort, we can change the patterning established in childhood.

Just need to interrupt here, sorry. We could have addressed this earlier, but now is a perfect time to consider the place that your current scientific thinking has in our exploration of the true nature of the Universe. You do realize that all is known on a cosmic level, do you not? What constitutes a scientific breakthrough is really just the announcement of a tiny portion of what is and what always has been. In other words, your scientific advancement is merely your current bird's-eye view of the totality of the cosmos. We would not want to limit our discussion to only those ideas verified by your current and very limited state of scientific knowledge, would we? No, that type of discussion would not be worthy of our energy.

Easy for you to say, Mister Pliny the Know-It-All Elder! Coming from your position of knowing it all, I would probably say the same thing. But we humans don't have the whole big picture. We—or I should say I—need to hang onto something from the material world to make sense of the nonmaterial. I, for one, am willing to jump off into the nonphysical but please, may I have a grounding cord to the material world? Science—or, if you prefer, the current state of scientific understanding—gives me the connection I need. I look for scientific evidence that supports my view of the metaphysical. It gives me the security I need to venture into the unknown.

Well! We certainly got you going there, didn't we? This is the type of spirited discourse we've been hoping to engender. No need to hold back. This is why we've chosen you, Dear One, as the medium for our project: Your innate feistiness which has been too long under wraps.

We see you get sidetracked by a text message and would again ask for your undivided attention. We are working here, although we like to call it play. And the fact that it's play in no way diminishes its importance. So PLEASE, put the phone away. Nothing is more important than our time together. Nothing!

Okay, in the future the phone will be tucked away out of sight.

Entitlement

Here's an important PS for you: Throughout the day, we ask you to focus on the idea of your entitlement. This is a word that usually has a negative connotation. But the truth is, from a cosmic standpoint, you are entitled to everything your soul desires. And it is the cause of much of the world's ills to NOT RECOGNIZE THIS! Sorry, we don't mean to shout. It's just that this concept is SO IMPORTANT and so few of you get it.

I'm starting to get it. As a matter of fact, *A Course in Miracles* says that too, in workbook Lesson 77 which states "I am entitled to miracles" (*A Course in Miracles Workbook* 1975, 137).

We are glad they are affirming this important truth. A question to ask yourself would be how to embody miracles in your own life every day, including the completely miraculous healing of your consciousness which in turn leads to bodily healing.

Spiritual Awakening

I've been reading again, Pliny.

> *Yes, we noticed that. You've been keeping your curious mind busy, haven't you? Ken Wilber,* The Ra Material? *Next, you'll be inquiring as to how many angels can dance on the head of a pin.*

But the book I'm reading now, *Extraordinary Awakenings* by Steve Taylor, is helpful in a practical, not just theoretical, way. The author, a psychotherapist, recounts the life stories of his patients who have undergone spiritual awakenings as a result of trauma such as war or imprisonment. One feature common to all of the awakenings is that they were preceded by what I now recognize as a shift into quantum consciousness and a loss of their attachment to their separate selves, their bodies, and their own personal concerns. It occurred to me that I would welcome a new perspective like that. It would be a relief because I get kind of bored with my own problems. I've been over the same territory so many times. There don't seem to be any new and exciting solutions coming from my habitual ways of thinking about myself and my illness.

> *We would agree that less focus on your illness would be helpful. You're familiar with the saying "Energy flows where attention goes"? Yes, you are. And while that certainly is true, we also would like to remind you that you are occupying a body, where self-centeredness and obsession with the physical is an occupational hazard. Our goal is not to chastise but merely save you and our Dear Readers eons of needless suffering. When one forgives oneself for any and all presumed transgressions related to focusing on the physical, or any topic for that matter, and gets on with the quantum jumping, suffering is minimized. We vote for that.*

That feels so good and comforting too. I see that I'm pretty hard on myself sometimes.

Sometimes? Ah hahaha.

The Holographic Universe

I have another question that I think is related to quantum thinking. I'm trying hard, but not really understanding what is meant by the concept of the "holographic Universe."

This terminology is merely a way for those on the material plane to describe the relationship of the individual to the whole. All the elements of the Universe are in you, and you are reflected in all the elements of the Universe. It is not an easy concept to comprehend with one's thinking brain, which is true for most quantum concepts. But don't despair, we've just gotten a bit muddled, haven't we? A very good reason to stop thinking.

When I was reading a James Redfield book years ago, I received an image that is helpful for me in evoking that unity feeling: The Universe is an egg suspended in space and I am sitting on top of the egg.

Yes, it works for you, and that's what counts. Here is our suggestion for an enhancement to that image: Picture yourself opening up the egg and walking inside. Once there, you will understand that there is truly no "outside" and no "inside." It's just all of one piece and beyond all words to describe.

Mood and Healing

I'm hoping you'll be able to get through today, Pliny. I've been feeling very poorly since my last COVID-19 vaccine and need a little pick-me-up from your side.

Yes, we know you've been feeling a bit downtrodden and have been sending you some lighthearted playful ideas in the form of puppy butts and the like. We find it very odd how the right puppy butt can transform your whole day. Did you enjoy these messages, Dear One?

Yes, I enjoyed them and felt enlivened several times but still slunk into the gloom and stayed there most of the weekend. Basically, I was unable to take my puppy outside and he pooped all over my house.

We are sorry to hear that. We find it difficult to broadcast to you when you've slunk into the gloomy swamp. Perhaps we will try writing at a later time today. Meanwhile we are going to be transmitting more upbeat messages to you to get you in a better reference range to hear our transmissions.

Pliny, please just talk to me. Say the truth about how things are. Just hold forth. I'm listening and eager to hear whatever comes through.

It's not so much a question of how things are, but how YOU are, because, you see, you are a fractal of the cosmos, and it is your consciousness that creates the things and conditions of your life. Primacy of consciousness, as mentioned before, is the name of the game. If your consciousness is a gloomy swamp, so is your life. You've just created what we will refer to as "Camp Swampy." AND you can never leave. Never, that is, until you alter your consciousness.

Hmm, Camp Swampy is a very familiar place to me. Visits are often preceded by feelings of shame, of incorrectness, which cause me to withdraw, hold my tongue, and be overly cautious. I'm usually thinking that there's one right way to do something, and I obviously don't know what that is.

And that doesn't feel good, does it? No, it's exhausting. Dear One is feeling like taking a nap and she's only just woken up.

Exactly!

[The next day]

We are here to proclaim the newness of this new day (insert drawing of megaphone). Dear One needn't rely on the tracks she laid down yesterday. After all, those tracks lead directly to Camp Swampy.

So, then, blaze a new trail this morning, one that leads to the summit overlooking the swamp. There, you can review all you thought you ever knew. There, you can turn around 180 degrees and overlook a completely new vista, or perhaps you choose to turn twenty-seven degrees and overlook a partially new vista. Yes, you are experiencing a quantum perspective now where you are not limited to a mere 360 degrees. You now have an infinite number of degrees to choose from. Are you appreciating this grand viewpoint as much as we are?

Um, well, I think I'm still in Camp Swampy. I don't really know how to blaze a trail to the summit.

We cannot do it for you, but we can assure you that we will be strewing breadcrumbs on the trail in subsequent conversations, so please pay attention. Also, we will endeavor to come through with ideas about how to affect a new upward trajectory in your meditation this morning.

Pliny, in an effort to get out of Camp Swampy I just listened to an interview with Sheila Gillette channeling an entity named Theo. Theo's explanation of "soul integration" and the importance of integrating parts of the self that had become frozen over time was especially helpful to me.

Dear One always feels comforted when an "expert" corroborates our teachings. We are looking forward to the day she learns to trust our channeled wisdom as much or perhaps even more than that of the "experts."

Karma

I do trust your wisdom, Pliny, but I also have other trusted sources of truth, Noa being the primary one. She has said that my current disease manifestation is the result of ancestral or perhaps past-life karma and is not the result of life lessons from my current lifetime. Can you enlighten me?

We would say to you, again, that your attempt to differentiate between the current lifetime with your current biological lineage or past lifetimes is of very little practical value and, from our cosmic vantage point, makes no actual sense whatsoever. You are aware, we know, that linear time is a construct of the material world and has no relation to anything in the quantum. Time merely serves to organize events for those experiencing a physical incarnation. We will, however, observe that one of your primary agreements prior to incarnating into this body was to heal your biological ancestral lineage of the fear that had become so predominant. There is still much work to be done in this area, although we want to give you a big SHOUT OUT for your herculean efforts. (Please insert megaphone drawing here.)

Soul Purpose

Dear One's mind is "Chock Full o'Nuts" today. And, for the benefit of our younger readers who have no idea what we're talking about, Chock Full o'Nuts was a brand of coffee popular in days gone by. We have no idea why it was called that, and we don't care.

You're right, I'm feeling kind of nutty today. I'm thinking about how I was too preoccupied with other things to really be a good mom to my daughter, Christy, when she was a child. What prompted this line of thinking was that Lani, the little dog I was dog sitting for yesterday, jumped off my second-story balcony while I was in the kitchen cooking chili. Luckily, she was unhurt (a miracle?). But I kept playing a tape of what might have happened had we not been so lucky.

Ahem, we would like to point out here that luck had no part in this jumping incident. Our little Lani was gently deposited on the lawn under your balcony with angelic intervention.

I was wondering about that. I was trying to figure what the chances were of a small dog hurling herself off a second-story balcony and not breaking any bones, not even stubbing one tiny toe.

Here is a good "jumping off point" for another of our profound pronouncements: Chance plays no part in any of these earthly occurrences. Nada. Zilch. Zippo. You and all your fellow travelers currently in bodies are constantly calling forth and experiencing the circumstances and events that best fulfill your respective purposes—your soul's purpose. Perhaps in parallel Universes other variations are occurring so you can try those on for size, but we really don't want to address the parallel lives question here, although it's a topic advanced physicists love to argue about. But the honest truth is that you, Dear One, can't understand it with your mind so it's not worth taking up bandwidth to consider. It's just what's so. Suffice it to say that all of the happenings and out-picturings in your physical world stem from choices, be they conscious or subconscious, which arise from the soul's desire for perfection. Thus, they are perfect choices for your present situation, even those that appear unfortunate on a physical level, including your daughter Christy's choice of you as her mother AND the dog leaping incident. Absolute perfection!

How Animals Assist Humans

Ah, the dog arriveth!

Dear One is dog sitting again today, determined to make up for yesterday by keeping a close eye on the little one. The dog spirit that is Lani has come forth in service to her owner, the personality known as Betty. Lani has agreed to reflect the conditions present in Betty's nervous system. Lani is actually taking on some of Betty's characteristics in order for Betty to see and heal them. Trauma, resultant anxiety, desperation, and hopelessness are all embodied in Lani's behavior.

Abandonment and ensuing panic feelings arise in the dog's body. These, Dear One, are feelings you too know well. Just try some deep breathing and little Lani will calm down. See? She has stopped the involuntary shaking. She wants to be close to you but then gets nervous at being thus contained. Vocalizing helps her diffuse the nervous tension. You may want to sing along. That is all for today, Dear One. We will be with the spirit of Lani in her dear little dog body.

Addictions

With your permission, I'd like to discuss a problem that I can't seem to find a solution for.

We would not affirm the proposition that you have any problems at all because, in truth, you have none. Try accessing your expanded self which sees all and knows all. That should clear things up. But, please, speak to us of what is troubling you. We will assist you in accessing your right mind.

I have been aware and troubled by a growing dependence on my digital devices. You've told me before that this is an addiction and is therefore unhealthy, but I feel helpless to make any lasting changes.

We believe we've said this before, but it bears repeating. In finding solutions to addictive behavior, or any unwanted behavior for that matter, it is important to first be in your right mind. That is, to be in your expanded self. That is where all solutions lie. Solutions coming from the ego mind are not viable solutions. It will steer you wrong every time with the directive "seek but do not find." (Insert image of dog barking up the wrong tree.) Ask, instead, your Soul Self who has known you and loved you since before the beginning of time. That one knows the sources of your misperceptions and has solutions uniquely tailored to effectively heal them.

Please ask your Soul Self if changing your behavior is something that will benefit you. If the answer is yes, ask how that may best be accomplished. When you have done that, please report back to us.

Do it now?

Yes, we can think of no better time.

Okay, so I did get some insight into the nature of the problem and maybe into the solution as well. I got that I use my phone to insulate me from uncomfortable feelings. Often that feeling seems like boredom but perhaps the boredom is just a placeholder for general not-okayness with present conditions, whatever dissatisfaction might be prevailing at that moment.

Very good, Dear One!

The Quantum Field

I found I was able to stop the compulsive behavior when I engaged my Soul Self as a witness. And I do feel a subtle difference in the smoothness of the field, and by *field* I mean that ambient frequency running in the background of my consciousness, humming my own personal little hum. Or maybe that IS my consciousness. Whatever that is, it feels a little less choppy to me, and I'm picturing the ocean surface, just in case you can't read my mind.

> *Rest assured; we are skilled in reading your mind. Or we should say we don't have to read your mind because we ARE your mind. This concept that physicists call the quantum field bears some discussion. And you're going to have to just let go of the reins right now because I'm going to put some stuff out there that the personality that is Joy isn't aware of.*

> *Yes, the quantum field is generated by the experience of consciousness of the ALL, and that would be the big A, big double L, which includes a whole lot, you see. And what we would say next is going to blow your panties off, to use a favorite expression of Dear One's friend, the lively and loving spirit known as Mauryne. The quantum field is the framework for everything and everybody that ever was or will be. It is the bowl that holds the quantum soup as well as all the ingredients in the soup. To make it more relevant to the physical plane, you may think of the ingredients in the soup as the individualized fractals of consciousness that you distinguish and name as individual people or things.*

Well, that didn't blow my panties off, Pliny. You're going to have to do better than that.

Language and Duality

We hate to tell you, but there is nothing better than that. But we're running into linguistic problems here because "better" is a comparative idea which, in turn, presupposes dualism. So now we are singing the song from Porgy and Bess "It ain't Necessarily So," and we would leave it at that because to say the notion of duality is false would again affirm a dualistic point of view.

Wow, you can hardly say anything then without getting into the duality territory, can you?

Exactly, and to expand upon that further, it makes absolutely no sense, on the quantum level anyway, to distinguish between duality and nonduality. The concept of nonduality points to an inclusive quantum state whereas the languaged word nonduality is inherently dualistic by virtue of its naming. This seeming paradox is, in a nutshell, the problem with using language to convey Truth. But in the material world, where precious few souls are conversant in quantum speak, it's pretty much all we've got, so we will carry on using it.

In the quantum world, the non-dual state is evidenced by the fact that photons can be both here and not here, a non-dual situation if there ever was one. Quantum physicists are able to give only a percentage of probability that photons are at one place rather than another at any point in time. Further complicating the picture is the fact that observation or measurement of those fickle little critters (the photons) changes their state from a wave to a particle. Here, the wave state could be described as a condition including all possibilities, whereas the act of observation or measurement would bring human consciousness into the picture, and the wave would collapse into a particle of matter. This

*is the basis of the primacy of consciousness hypothesis that
will soon be universally accepted as Truth.*

*Because the quantum is a both/and rather than an either/or
paradigm, it is futile to expect constructive results from
social or political debates based on material world thinking
which includes right/wrong, good/bad, crazy/sane. And we
could go on ad nauseum but will not.*

Problem Solving and the Quantum

*It is apparent that no good solutions to the world's
problems have been or will be forthcoming from discussions
on a dualistic level. A shift (jump) to quantum thinking is
required if humanity wishes to continue to evolve. The
inability of humans to access quantum consciousness is one
important reason for the political and social disruptions of
recent years. However, since COVID-19 forced the world
to press the pause button, souls are waking up to the
possibilities presented by a paradigm shift that includes
quantum ideas. They are ready to join together with other
newly awakened souls and apply their higher-level consciousness to the problems facing the Earth and its people,
and just in time, we would say.*

Sense of Oneness

I just noticed that recently my meditations are originating from an
underlying "we" perspective rather than a "me" perspective. Since
I've been talking to you, Pliny, everything in my physical world is
presenting me with the idea of oneness, these past few days
especially.

*Yes, and we would go so far as to say that the reason you've
chosen the word presenting is that it's a gift. How
reassuring for you, to know that you're not alone as you
walk the ways of the material world, that in the quantum*

realm is all the support and assistance you could ever need. This awareness is especially valuable because it shows you exactly how you may be of service and reaffirms that you and your fellow beings and even insentient objects are one. You know that there are no idle thoughts, and because thoughts create things, you can bring solace, and even salvation, to other souls in the world by affirming and experiencing the oneness of all creation.

Cause and Effect

Did I just hear you say that thoughts create things? Doesn't that mean that things are caused by thoughts?

Yes, that would be the logical conclusion to be drawn by one in the physical world. But from a quantum perspective, it goes like this: Things (matter and events) arise spontaneously based on conditions at the local (physical) level. Let us leave it at that and not worry it further. Be comforted by the fact that this is a concept that's near impossible for you to grasp with your thinking mind. Meanwhile, we see that Dear One has chosen to eat her lunch during our session. These complex topics are best left to a time when we have your full attention. We will speak further about this seeming conundrum in later conversations.

Chapter 4
More on Quantum Physics

Cause, Effect, and Time

To continue and elaborate on the topic of cause and effect, we can add yet one more idea, namely, time. We have established that on the cosmic level, where there is no time (i.e., past, present, and future), events do not unfold in a sequential order so it would be impossible for one event to happen as a result of another, would it not?

Quantum physicists are now positing a looping type of self-reflective reality…

Whoa! Slow those horses down. They're going into the ditch. We don't want Dear One to regurgitate so-called facts again, do we? With no disrespect toward her considerable innate human intelligence, we would say that it is difficult for her to understand logically many of these advanced concepts. Let us just say that the lack of causality and sequential time on the cosmic level are just "what's so." Your inability to conceive of the lack of them does not in any way disprove their "what's so-ness."

Free Will

I've been thinking, Pliny...

A very dangerous activity.

Yes, I know, but let me get this out. It feels important. It's about free will.

[Sigh]. Here we go again with the compression and contortion of Dear One's gray matter.

You know how long I've been wrestling with the concept of free will? All my life, really, I've given a lot of time and attention to the question of whether it does or doesn't exist. It almost seems like it's the subject of a koan (a zen riddle designed to promote quantum thinking) I've been given. If I figure it out, I get the prize, which I think may be enlightenment. If I don't figure it out, I get the chute, which is samsara (the never-ending cycle of birth, death, and rebirth without awakening). Since I've met you, Pliny, I've concluded that free will does, indeed, exist but only on the quantum level. On the physical plane you're pretty circumscribed by your conscious and subconscious conditioning, no?

Here's where we pause for one giant deep breath—several, if you prefer. The problem with discussing abstract topics from a conceptual point of view is that there is very little translation from one mind to the next due to varying perceptions and the problems inherent in language itself. Words mean different things to different people. We can talk theoretically about free will till those beautiful cows come home, but it may not translate well to individual experience.

We would prefer to consider those cows, the ones off grazing in some lush green Alpine pasture. We see and hear a babbling brook nearby. The cows are so content munching the grass and enjoying the sunshine that they are disinclined to come home. Who wants to be confined in a stall, having someone pulling on their teats?

Sorry to be so graphic here Dear One, but we want you to get the full picture and the experience of roaming freely in the grass as compared to being cooped up in the cow shed. Granted, the cow shed provides shelter from inclement weather, so we can't take this metaphor too far, but we find it helpful to liken the freedom of will in roaming the pasture to being in a state of expanded consciousness where all possible realities may be entertained. It is in this state that your concept of free will exists. Here you are free to cocreate with God and revel in that exhilarating atmosphere of dynamic creativity. Oh, how delicious! (Please insert a drawing of a contented cow.)

This is what we as discarnate energies experience all the time. This is why souls who have near-death experiences (NDEs) are disinclined to come back to the physical world. Now, at some point, those cows do come home, just as souls on the physical plane will choose a course of action, leading to a collapse of the waveform of all possibilities and leading to the creation of molecules which combine to form solid matter. But it was fun being wavy for a while, wasn't it Dear One?

Soul Contracts

Yes, Pliny, I enjoyed grazing the meadows with you. But here's another idea related to free will—

I thought we had laid that to rest in the cow shed.

I've read that free will is limited even in the quantum world because of soul contracts that individual personalities make before they incarnate. Is this true?

Now we're on the horns of a dilemma. (Please insert a drawing of cow horns here.) You are asking whether the proposition is true or false. And our answer is yes. As we have said before, dualistic propositions such as true/false make no sense in the quantum reality. Let us just affirm that individuals have complete freedom to interpret soul contracts as they suit their soul purposes. They exercise their free will in altering, postponing, or otherwise changing them in any way they see fit. We know this answer may not be satisfying to Dear One, who is still caught up in dualistic thinking.

Not at all, Pliny. I'm feeling very satisfied.

A caveat: The above explanation of free will was filtered through Dear One's consciousness and is very rudimentary in nature although basically correct. Here we are running up against not only the strictures of language but also Dear One's limited knowledge of math and science. Humans have spent much time in needless mentation and fruitless dentation on the subject of free will. We deem it preferable to go back to the pasture where the sun is so warm, and we feel so free.

Okay, so I got that on the material level you're pretty much run by your subconscious conditioning; that is, every choice you make is based on those mostly negative and mostly untrue stories you tell yourself. However, when you transcend the material level, that is, when you begin to be quantumly conscious, you begin to free up your possibilities.

First of all, you're able to forgive yourself for past mistakes, realizing that you were making those choices based on your material world consciousness. When you're able to transcend the ego, free will can become part of the operating system because it begins to dawn on you that you have the choice to either heap shame and blame upon yourself and everyone involved OR you can choose the love and forgiveness route that includes zero pain and suffering. This is where your free will comes into play. You see that your will IS God's will, and you see you have the opportunity to choose again and take a different route.

By Jove, we think she's got it! We are so glad you are hearing our words and ideas so clearly. We do need to say, as an aside here, that until a human is ready to listen to the "good news," they're not ready to hear the "good news." Now, all that is required is a bit of practice in this type of listening, and by "a bit," we mean every nanosecond for the rest of your long and beautiful life. That is not too much to ask, is it?

Astrology and Free Will

Pliny, I don't want to throw a wrench into our already finely tuned free will explanation, but during an astrology reading I had yesterday, my astrologer friend said that humans have a lot less free will than they like to think they do. He said that one master astrologer told him that it was an 80/20 deal, that is, 80 percent of one's life is predetermined based on pre-birth soul contracts as well as social and emotional conditioning and the like, which leaves only 20 percent free will. What do you think of that?

We don't think much of it.

No, I'm really interested in this topic. Do you think this theory is true?

Yes, we do think it's true, as is every other possible number from one to one hundred, assuming the whole is 100 percent. What the probabilities are is another story. Do you like the idea of having only 20 percent free will?

No, not especially.

Then don't choose that option. Choose a number that suits you better. Or, better yet, picture the life you have when you are exercising your free will. Picture it, smell it, taste it, hear it. Then jump into the picture and feel the emotions connected with it. Is that not infinitely more satisfying?

Yes, and it also occurred to me that astrologers might have a tendency to believe in predestination because of their training in which the planets exert a huge influence on the lives of humans. It would predispose them to think in terms of predestination, wouldn't it?

Right again, Dear One!

Purpose of This Book and Creation

I've been wondering about the purpose of this book. I think that writing it is very therapeutic for me, but is it also intended to help other people dealing with their illnesses?

We have never set out to write a medical treatise, nor are we prescribing a course of action for those seeking healing.

What are we doing then?

It is an ongoing creation, one example of how the larger process of creation works. In order to explain this, we will have to delve into some advanced ideas.

Delve away.

You have had the idea that there is some separate deity "out there" that is calling the shots. He (please forgive our gender non-neutrality) has a predetermined, predestined, future in store for all you poor peons in his thrall.

Umm, yeah, I kind of do believe that.

We are here to tell you that just isn't the way it works.

The truth is that you, as a part of the cosmic consciousness and the All That Is (another name for God), are making it up as you go along. Yup, flying by the seat of your collective cosmic pants. Winging it, if you prefer. You and all the other holographic fractals are cocreating the whole shebang.

All this sounds very random and chaotic; does it not? Well, nothing could be further from the truth. Your physical creations, including everything you have manifested on the physical plane, arise from, guess what? Your consciousness! Consciousness allows for the creation of what scientists are calling "thought forms" or "morphic fields." They are, in essence, placeholders where information is stored. They serve as templates for the elegantly intelligent generation of physical matter.

Placebo and Nocebo Effects

We are mentioning this theory only because it can be very helpful in the human understanding of disease creation. When doctors give an unfavorable prognosis to a patient regarding the course of their illness, it can be very counterproductive because the doctor's words create a thought field, which, unless countered by some heavy-duty deconditioning, can result in the creation of a disease with an unfavorable outcome, up to and including death. This is, in a nutshell, the mechanism underlying the nocebo effect. Of course, it also accounts for the placebo effect, which has an equally high probability of effectiveness. The more one experiences quantum living, the higher the degree of probability.

Wow! That's very encouraging. Right now, I'm reading Shamini Jain's book, *Healing Ourselves,* and she does a wonderful job of unpacking the complexity of the placebo effect. Can I tell you about that?

You have our undivided attention.

She describes what are called "open label" research studies in which participants are told they are being given placebos and are also educated about how effective placebos are. This type of study directly tests the effectiveness of the *idea* of placebo as a treatment modality. As might be expected, the participants who received the placebos and were informed about the effectiveness of placebos ahead of time fared better than participants who weren't told about the effectiveness of placebos or that they would be receiving placebos. This straightforward study pulls the curtain away and, the real wizard is revealed. It's the placebo effect! Don't you love it?

We do, indeed, but it might be more accurate to say that it is the energy behind the placebo that is the wizard, and it is really nothing more or less than the power of human consciousness. It also pulls the curtain away from the false notion that illness is caused by outside agents, something that is not you. By placing the responsibility in its rightful place—smack dab in the center of you—you're able to respond to it and heal it. The implications of the placebo effect put you, Dear One, in a central position of power, where you have always been, but which you have denied.

Disease Progression

Doctors can predict the probability of a particular outcome; however, without some shift at the local level, such as a change of perspective on the part of the host (hint, hint), the illness will most likely progress on the path of probability predicted by the data.

Do you remember that ground-breaking work Mind as Healer, Mind as Slayer *by Kenneth Pelletier? Yes, you do. It was written over forty years ago, but Pelletier was onto something big way back then. Now, scientists are providing scientific evidence in the form of data from experiments to validate Pelletier's hypothesis that the mind, in the form of thoughts and emotions, does, indeed, affect matter. Science is beginning to understand how this happens, that is, how consciousness produces the biomolecular environment that creates the local conditions that give rise to the material. Stay with us. Are you following?*

Yes, go on.

The big takeaway here, and we're not talking about fast food, is that there is no predetermined outcome for your cancer. So stop with the envisioning of a future you don't want. Sure, there are some probabilities, but there's also the good news that you can affect those probabilities with your consciousness. Just remember those contented cows and the Puppy Poo Principle and you'll be fine.

How to Take Medication

Thank you. That is very good news. With your permission, I'd like to tell a story about that very thing, that is, the power of consciousness to affect matter. It's pretty important, I think.

Certainly. Proceed. You don't need our permission. As Shauna keeps reminding you, this is YOUR book.

As you know, I just started taking a new medication for my leukemia last week, and I was having trouble tolerating it, which is med-speak for "sick as a dawg and can't get up off the bathroom floor." You get the picture.

Yes, we know the full extent of your suffering because we were there on the floor with you the whole time.

Well, Noa came over the next morning, and showed me how to bless the pill. Here are the steps:

Put the pill in the center of your hand and take several deep belly breaths, expanding your abdomen but with your chest and shoulders hardly moving. Feel the energetic pulse of the pill in your hand. Then, picture divine energy circulating around and through your heart and into the pill. Do that several times, the idea being that the blast of purified energy removes all unpleasant effects as well as any greed or self-serving motives connected with the development, marketing, and administration of the pill.

This leaves the pill in its pristine state, consisting of only natural elements which come from the Earth. Just like you and me. Well, me anyway.

> *We would remind you that we are of the Earth too, but just not limited to the Earth and neither are you. But go on with your story. Although we know the outcome, we can't wait for others to hear it.*

Well, while I was performing this ritual, I intuited that the pill's name was Callie, which comes from her trade name, Calquence, and that the two of us would be friends and that, in fact, we already were friends. We would have a mutually supportive and rewarding relationship. I would recognize her not as an unconscious, inert substance, but as a friend who wanted to help me heal. And by telling this story to others, I would enable her and her sister (and brother) pills to be more helpful to more people and avoid the kind of agony I experienced on the bathroom floor the other night. She would also assist me by showing me the ego stories that created the disease in the first place. In short, she would assist in my healing, and we would be in service to each other and humanity.

> *Quite so. See how far you advanced in your knowledge of self in the space of several days? From the poor thing on the bathroom floor to being in service to humanity. It is truly miraculous.*

> *You are correct in your assumption that the same pro-cedures outlined above will, with perhaps a few minor adjustments, work well when applied to other medications and treatments, some of which can be put in the palm of one's hand and some which cannot. Truth be told, which it always is by us, the same procedures can be applied to*

almost any substance or situation calling for rectification of energy.

Can we call that the "Callie Procedure"?

You may call it whatever you like.

Chapter 5
The Purpose of Illness

Can you feel our energy through the hand that is doing the writing? Yes, we thought so. You are questioning why you have never noticed this sensation before, and we will tell you that our energy is running strongly, like your industrial sewing machine that refused to turn off this morning. Even when you turned the switch to the clearly marked OFF position, that big workhorse of a machine refused to be led to the barn. It just kept humming its deep-throated hum, didn't it?

Yes, it did. I finally had to pull the plug on it.

We would exhort you: Please promise not to pull the plug on us... Ah hahaha.

I promise.

Another factor is in play here (note: the deliberate choice of the word play).

Ever since we spent that time working out themes by which to organize our book, you are very much in tune with us. You are now exquisitely sensitized to us because you have tuned your instrument to the exact frequency of the entity known as Pliny. Might it be 440 hertz, the frequency that most orchestras around the world tune their stringed instruments to? It might be, but in actuality it is not. We are just using that frequency as an example so that Dear One— herself an amateur violinist—will understand.

In this chapter we will address the question, What is the purpose of illness? And please don't get too far ahead of us now. We have the reins and are directing those horses, remember?

Firstly, we are glad of Dear One's acceptance of and, yes, enthusiasm for the topic known as quantum physics. In chapters three and four, we covered this complex subject in a very rudimentary way, mostly from a philosophical point of view, and primarily as it relates to health and disease. Without at least a basic grasp of the quantum perspective, illness makes no sense whatsoever.

Nay, we misspoke once again.

Please allow us to restate the previous sentence, for it is at the root of what has been called the hard problem of consciousness, which questions where consciousness comes from in the first place. Without an understanding of the quantum principle that consciousness creates matter, illness does not make good sense. The cause of illness might be attributed to bad luck or a vengeful god or both, in any case, a most unfriendly Universe.

This is not a pleasant scenario to contemplate, is it? No, it is not, and we want to reassure you that this unpleasant view is not based in Truth (capital T).

When the brilliant and evolutionary physicist Albert Einstein asked if the Universe is a friendly place, he intuitively knew the right answer but wasn't able to make the mathematics come out right in order to prove it. He wrestled with the problem for years, and it was supremely frustrating to him. Modern physicists, with their primacy of consciousness theory, are now enabling us to understand what Einstein couldn't.

Pliny, I feel called to interrupt here because I want to talk about what *A Course in Miracles (ACIM)* says about this issue. It says that the purpose of illness is to demonstrate that although I have a body, from a cosmic perspective I am *not* a body. I'm a spirit that is free to be as I was created by God; that is to say, complete, whole, and healed in every way. Inherent in this idea, however, is the idea that I'm also free to continue to be ill, if that is what I choose. The *ACIM* view of illness points to the possibility and perhaps necessity of transcending the physical in order to heal the body.

We are not as happy with the idea of transcendence as Dear One is. We know that ACIM has led her out of some very tall weeds; but we would say, in the interest of full disclosure, that we do not resonate as resoundingly with ACIM as she does. We like to think of the body not as something to be transcended but a precious, valuable, one-of-a-kind vehicle (in her case, a vintage vehicle, ah hahaha), that always takes her where she wants to go.

And how grateful are we for that? Beyond measure, we would say. But here we also affirm that the Truth is true, and, whether or not one resonates with the vehicle idea, is related to one's ambient frequency. For example, Dear One prefers the macadamia nut crunch flavored ice cream, whereas we, the entity known as Pliny, prefer the pistachio. We think that might be due, at least in part, to its lovely mint green color. But since we are not in favor of overanalysis, shall we just go ahead and partake in this ice cream before it melts?

Shauna is calling for clarification of the ice cream image. She likes ice cream too but is wondering how it relates to the idea of resonance and frequency mentioned just prior. What we mean to say is that although "all roads lead to Rome," individuals can reach that designation in a variety of ways. For example, one person might take the freeway while another might prefer the back roads. Dear One resonates more with ACIM ideas than we, the entity known as Pliny, do.

Let us spell it out in even further detail. Individuals vibrate in their own unique way and have their own ambient frequency. Dear One's vibration is such that she is open to the wisdom inherent in ACIM and has benefited greatly from studying it over the years. We, on the other hand, have not experienced that same benefit, so are not as attuned to its frequency. That does not in any way negate the Truth that ACIM points to. Just think of it as a road sign pointing to the final destination, Rome. The Truth is true no matter how you get there.

Clear?

As crystal. Thank you. I don't want to overanalyze things, but I'm not quite finished with this topic yet.

Last night I listened to one of my favorite podcasts, Buddha at the Gas Pump, and the person being interviewed was an *ACIM* scholar. Much of the conversation was about just this topic, the role of the body in spiritual development. The scholar was describing the body as an illusion created by the egoic mind. Is that true?

Yes, it is True (capital T) and also not true (small t). Here, the capital T represents Truth from a non-dual or quantum perspective and the small t represents truth as it exists as part of dichotomy which characterizes the material world. From a material perspective, it is downright silly to say the body is an illusion, is it not? Certainly, for those living in pain and suffering, the body seems very real. And from that perspective one might, indeed, judge the proposition to be false. From a quantum perspective, however, the body is the manifestation of the ego's thoughts about its corporeality and is thus an illusion. From this perspective, the proposition is True.

Clear?

Not really, can you say more?

A Course in Miracles is a program designed to retrain the mind to jump directly from the material to the quantum, and in doing so has been the salvation of many a sufferer. Where we would have one slight quibble with ACIM, and you know that we are not normally quibblesome, is that humans tend not to be consistently quantumly conscious, a state which is rare to nonexistent in the general population, and we find it most unhelpful to suppose otherwise.

The sweet spot here is the place that acknowledges both your physicality and your divinity, for it is there that your best work can be done. You can acknowledge all the Truth contained in A Course in Miracles which says that the body is a wholly neutral thing whose only True purpose is communication, and at the same time benefit from the lessons that are to be learned through both the pleasure and adversity inherent in living in a body. We will add an important postscript to this topic: It is ever so much easier, quicker, and more pleasurable to learn these lessons from an expanded state of love and forgiveness than from the contracted state of negativity from which most humans operate.

That sounds like a typical Pliny response. You are saying both ideas about the body are true, that it can be seen both as real and an illusion, depending on where you're coming from.

That sounds good to us. No need to make anyone wrong.

76

We are still considering the topic called "the purpose of illness," are we not? Yes, we thought so.

Do you remember the erudite and profound pronouncement we put forth in which we said, "The purpose of time is to figure out the purpose of time"? Yes, we know it has been said before by other equally erudite entities, and yes, we know it is a circular definition and frowned upon by academics, but we remind you of it here because the same line of reasoning can be applied to the topic of illness.

Yes, the purpose of illness is to enable humans to piece together the reason for their illness and learn from it. You see, many, if not most, people—when they become sick—attribute their disorder to some cause on the material level (e.g., a bad oyster, that blasted A/C, Agent Orange, etc.). And yes, we would agree, those things have been shown to be associated with and even causative of illness on a physical level where cause and effect are in full swing. But on a quantum level, where cause and effect are not the law (and not even a good idea), we see that energy blockages arise spontaneously from unhappy thoughts and emotions and may contribute to the terrain from which seeds of illness sprout.

Are you saying it's my stinkin' thinkin' that's causing my illness?

No, we would never use those irreverent words, and we would not make those negative thoughts the villains because we know, beyond all doubt, that in your manifest world, they were absolutely and completely justifiable given the circumstances in which you found yourself. However, these unhappy thoughts, limiting beliefs, ego stories, lies, whatever you want to call them, are the precursors to the energy blockages from which illness arises. Notice we are taking great pains here to avoid using causation language because, as we've been repeating, cause and effect are not operational on a quantum level.

Dear One is now pulling on our collective toga, asking us if she may please include some content from current scientific literature that she feels will be helpful in illustrating our point? Agreed.

One name comes immediately to mind in connection with the topic of body/mind connection: Bruce Lipton. Lipton is a biochemist and cell biologist who conducted laboratory experiments using human stem cells to show that the environment in which human stem cells were living, in this case culture medium, was responsible for turning on or off cellular genetic expression. This was big news because scientists had previously assumed that genes turned themselves on or off according to a theory called genetic determinism. Taking a huge leap from the petri dish to human consciousness and at the same time oversimplifying a very complex concept, research in this new field called epigenetics is showing that positive thoughts and beliefs are associated with health and well-being, the opposite being true for negative thoughts and beliefs.

This new field throws out the dirty dishwater of genetic determinism. Just because a person has a gene that predisposes them to a certain illness does not mean that the person will actually come down with it. Epigenetics tells us that it's the milieu or the environment in which the particles, molecules, or cells live that determines whether the bad-boy gene shows up in the physical. That's a big WHEW! and another example of the good news, and I can't tell you how happy I was to hear about it.

Although it is normally not our style to include information from Dear One's arsenal of scientific ammunition, we have agreed to discuss this information to support our previous profound pronouncement that disease arises from human consciousness, which includes emotions, thoughts, and beliefs.

Getting back to the original question regarding the purpose of illness, we would say that it frequently requires the actual experience of illness for humans to figure out the purpose of illness. Dear One is a poster child for this proposition. She was told she had cancer in 2010, and more than ten years later she is still deep in contemplation. At this point, she is on the verge of some profound conclusions of her own. She has loosened her grip on the idea that matter creates matter and is learning to sink into the Trust (insert drawing of a high-end mattress) that lies beyond her need for intellectual understanding. Can healing be far behind? We think not.

Sometimes I think I have the Truth nailed, and then later when doubts creep in I question, "can it really be my consciousness making me ill, or is that just wishful thinking?"

And then she prefers to blame the Roundup that she used on the weeds in the driveway in 1992 for her illness. The consciousness theory seems to her to be too simple to be true, to which we would rejoin, yes, simple, but not easy. Because, you see, the healing of the disease creation requires the dismantling of everything you thought you ever knew. It requires demolishing cherished notions and confronting yourself and your fears in a most fearless manner. But that's what you, Dear One, signed up for in this lifetime.

This amount of demolition that's involved requires a profound level of self-love and unquestioned acceptance of the God in you. It also requires constant vigilance. You must be alert to the presence of those unhappy, fear-based thoughts that are constantly sneaking up behind you with the chloroform-soaked rag. They do that all the time, you will agree! Before you can say Jack Robinson, they've put the darned thing over your mouth and nose, and you've gone unconscious again. Down, down, down the negative thought spiral you go. You're in the rabbit hole of unhappy thoughts, where, just like the Hotel California, you can check out, but you can't leave. Never, that is, until you wake up and jump out of the hole into the quantum.

In that last brief paragraph, we managed to use three very potent and pertinent analogies. Did you notice?

How could I not?

Quite so. The "waking up" part, the underlying impulse to jump out of the rabbit hole, is due to nothing more or less than what you term "grace," which we understand to be an unexpected and perhaps undeserved bestowing of blessing from a bountiful and ever-loving Universe, to which we can respond only by accepting and saying, "Thank you, God."

If you were to go so far as to sit down and pray, or maybe even go farther and kneel in prayer, your best bet would be to pray for the grace which would enable you to wake up. By praying for grace, you are not asking for any particular result or any specific manifestation in the physical, you are merely asking for your human birthright: The mercy of God, a.k.a. grace. In fact, we don't recommend praying for specific outcomes, although some do so with notable success. Once you are awakened, you can experience the expanded state where all is possible. There is your point of power where you have free will to choose your desired outcome. That is where you experience heaven on Earth.

I want to acknowledge those other two analogies you used, especially the chloroform-soaked rag one. Chloroform turns out to be highly carcinogenic so maybe that's what caused my cancer. The

"Hotel California" reference is also meaningful to those of us who listened to the Eagles in the 1970s. Well done, my friend!

Thank you for appreciating our evocative and colorful language. Now, please allow us to explain the purpose of illness from yet another quantum perspective. This perspective explains how your stories are directly connected to the purpose of your illness. We would like to recount a few more stories (notice we're not using the word lies, which is much more negatively charged) you tell yourself about your illness and illness in general.

We explained previously the falsehood of your perception that your illness is in some way related to your inherent incorrectness. Then, the question arises, What is the function of illness, from a cosmic perspective that is, if it is not related to anything incorrect? We notice that you're searching your brain cells for the answer to this stumper, and we think that here is where you're really going to have to let go of control, because your brain cells don't know the answer.

Illness arises in the context of the Universe's desire to expand itself through human experience. You are looking for that experience too, are you not? You want to create and embody your own unique flavor of experience that can come only through the vibration that is you. In your case, your human blueprint has predisposed you to do that through an exploration of physical illness. So, on a cosmic level, illness arises spontaneously as part of the human host's desire to fulfill their life's purpose.

Hmm. That's not going to be appreciated so much by people who are in pain and suffering. They probably feel very strongly that there's nothing purposeful or in any way positive about their illness and would prefer that God find some other way of expanding.

And we can only sigh a little and say, "Yes, you're right," because, of course, from our quantum vantage point, we recognize that if that is the way they see it, then that is what is true for them. It is only in the seeing of value in the illness experience that healing can and does begin, sometimes resolving all signs of disease in a nanosecond.

We would advise humans who want to heal their maladies to see them as opportunities to gain experience looking for evidence of their quantum nature, which Eastern traditions call their true nature, the all-knowing, all-powerful, all-loving being that they truly are. There is where so-called miracles occur—that pinpoint of light in the quantum fabric where the material intersects the cosmic, where the wave of possibility collapses into the creation of matter. The probability of miracles happening may be small, but happen they do. Yes, indeed-y. And when they do, those who are unconscious get to rethink everything they thought they knew. For those who have awakened, a miracle is a cause for much rejoicing, for it is further confirmation that what they know to be true is, indeed, True.

This is why we recommend reading about cases of radical remission of illness. Not only is it uplifting, but it also provides clues about the terrain from which miracles sprout. One would be wise to prepare one's own soil in a likewise manner. We are not speaking only metaphorically here. We would prescribe a bit of plant therapy for all those experiencing unwanted physical symptoms. The care and nurturing of plants can go a long way toward healing the body. We would refer you to our encyclopedic work on natural history, Naturalis Historia, *which contains much valuable and little-known information on plants. You have heard it from the horse's mouth: Buy some plants, put them in beautiful containers, water them, fertilize them. Listen to what they are asking for. Oh, and don't forget to sing to them every day. They like that and are an exceptionally non-critical audience. If you really feel you cannot or should not sing, then talking to them in a gentle way will do. Be sure to ask how they are feeling and if there is anything you may get for them. They will be surprisingly forthcoming.*

Dear One has recently had a discussion with her teacher, Noa, that included the topic which we are expounding upon currently: The purpose of illness. Since the evidence of the illness Dear One has created is in the form of enlarged lymph nodes, mainly in her neck, it is very easy for her to feel the evidence of her creation.

While I was on Noa's massage table the other day, I began to see my lymph nodes as little lost sheep which had gone astray. They had come to me with the best of intentions but had somehow gotten lost in the hills. Now, as a good shepherd, I am searching for them. I find them, round them up and, with the assistance of my faithful border collies, lovingly and without scolding, guide them back to the fold. They just needed to know that I loved them and understood why they wandered off in the first place. Now, they will be able to mingle and graze contentedly with the other sheep.

We like this visualization, mainly because of its gentleness, and would assert that good does not come from blame, shame, or recrimination of any kind. Also, it harkens the Christ archetype, with Christ as the good shepherd who is caring for his sheep and rescuing those animals who have gone astray. He welcomes them back into the fold (which we picture as a corral of sorts) without any judgment or grumbling. In this, Dear One is acting in a Christlike manner, of which we heartily approve. This treatise does not dwell on Christ nor mention much about Christianity or any other religion, but we would like it to be known that the Christ energy is in total alignment with our energy.

That's good to know. I feel that it is unfortunate how this loving, compassionate ethos has been twisted and generally misinterpreted through the ages by the Christian church which purports to represent His teachings, but which in Truth, has been more focused on advancing its own interests.

> *But enough of that! Although there is room in the quantum for every perspective, we are not in favor of soapboxes, except from a practical standpoint. They do come in handy for purposes such as storing and shipping boxes of detergent. Think of the mess you would have if there were no soap boxes in which to transport soap. We shudder in our togas at the thought.*

I've been thinking a lot lately about why my symptoms, mainly the lymph nodes in my neck, have not gone away. I feel like I'm on the right track, but they're still there. I must be doing something wrong. Am I not meditating enough?

> *You, Dear One, are an especially intrepid adventurer. You have signed up for a major shift in consciousness this lifetime. At the risk of sounding melodramatic, you have volunteered for the enlightenment track, and not the flash-in-the-pan enlightenment track either, rather the slow and steady enlightenment track. And you are exactly on schedule with your coursework. The lessons are not easy, but you would have it no other way.*

> *Regarding your question about the continuation of symptoms: You have signed up for a very intensive program which requires constant and conscientious practice. It requires you to be in an expanded state much of the time, focusing only on what makes you feel vital, alive, creative, and in love with yourself. When you are in that state, you are not in the least bit concerned about the size of your lymph nodes or your appearance, are you? Of course your lymph nodes are still enlarged. They're just loving all the*

attention and energy you've been giving them. When a child misbehaves, does it not work better to draw attention to something other than the source of the apparent problem, rather than heap shame and blame upon the child? The same tactic applies to your continued symptoms, you see. This is the most effective method of guiding them gently back to the fold.

Your challenge in this advanced curriculum is to focus on being in the expanded state and resist the temptation to assess the size of your lymph nodes and say, "Oh, it's not working. I must be doing something wrong." You—or, we should say, your ego—have no pony in this race and no frame of reference by which to evaluate the results of your practice. We, on the other hand, as the collective energy known as Pliny, are in a very good position to see the track. Although we will not give away the name of the winning pony, we will say that you, Dear One, are in a very good position against the rail.

Because I go to my oncologist every few months, during those weeks leading up to my blood test and appointment, I usually work myself up into a state of fear. Lately, however, since I've been channeling you, Pliny, I've not gotten as apprehensive as before.

And we are so glad of that. You see? Progress is being made in spite of your grim determination to hang on to the fear. In fact, it is you, Dear One, who is creating an outcome at every moment, with every thought and feeling you choose to entertain.

I was sure my white blood cell count would be thirty-five, and I spent time envisioning that number on the lab report and feeling euphoric when I received the results. But the number came back forty-five instead of thirty-five as I was intending. Why was that?

First of all, let us congratulate you on the fact that you received a lab report indicating that you are still alive. This is good news and cause for celebration, is it not? Second of all, we would like you to consider why this arbitrary number should have any bearing on how you feel, your level of fear, or your relationship to yourself and to God. Why should it have any effect on you at all? What we're getting at is this: The less you rely on outward appearances or circumstances to tell you how to experience your life, the better off you'll be. The reliance on blood tests or other rigamarole they put you through to determine whether to feel good or bad about yourself is sheer lunacy. Right now, doctors, lab results, and prognosticating tools have hijacked Dear One's sense of well-being. They have put a damper on her natural joie de vivre.

Yes, I'm aware that this is something I inflict on myself. It's a special hell of my own making, yet I haven't gotten enough traction in the skill of quantum jumping to be able to remedy the situation.

Traction? You are using the word traction and picturing one of those tractors with the gigantic tires you see at county fairs which are used in some testosterone-fueled competition, the purpose of which is God-only-knows what?

Yes, that's the image all right.

What if we were to suggest to you a more suitable image: A small white feather drifting on the breeze. That's the level of effort necessary to get the traction needed to jump into the quantum. The less concentrated your effort, the more successful the jump. It is, in fact, the same principle on which homeopathy is based. The less concentrated the remedy, the more powerful the effect.

Please, Dear One, stop all the "effort-ing." In general, we do not approve making a noun into another part of speech, such as a gerund like efforting, but it has meaning for Dear One, so we are making an exception. What we want to get across is that it takes not even the lightest touch of a feather or the brush of a butterfly wing to affect a change in the quantum. A simple photon formed as the result of a conscious thought will do the trick.

Everything I read tells me I could and should be doing more to cure my leukemia, such as rebounding, yoga, qigong, or changing my diet and taking supplements. How does all that fit into your healing model?

We would certainly not advise against them, but we emphasize that they should be undertaken only if they make you feel good, both physically and emotionally. Self-care routines can be very comforting and can contribute to healing to the degree that you believe they are helpful. The familiar placebo/nocebo effect is on duty twenty-four seven.

Regarding your symptoms and out-of-normal-range blood values: They are a result of erroneous thinking which has solidified into matter and is now manifesting as disease. Yes, all physical symptoms are downstream from the thoughts that created them.

This is a very juicy topic and warrants further discussion. The hijacking of your well-being by lab tests and doctor appointments, while not actual crimes, places you in the role of the victim. Do not accept that role. Your illness is the vehicle you chose in this lifetime to learn that you, in all your human imperfection, are perfectly lovable by dint of merely being alive. Once you have fully accepted and integrated this truth into your consciousness, the body will follow and the need for further teaching as well as the need for illness will fall away.

It is unfortunate that there are so few living examples of this principle in the world for people to follow. Of course, we know about the healings Jesus performed during biblical times, but there are precious few examples of miraculous healings currently being publicized.

There are, however, some notable exceptions I'd like to bring up. Anita Moorjhani's story of her miraculous recovery from cancer after a near-death experience is very compelling. She is one of my heroes not only because of her miraculous message, but also because of her low-key, humble demeanor. Her story has a resonance to it, and she has become very popular because people recognize its ring of Truth.

Anita's story confirms what other near-death experiencers have said, and that is, to die is a glorious event. Most, in fact, wanted to stay dead but returned to life only at the urging of some guide or other heavenly authority. Many have re-entered life with a newfound purpose, including the mission to inform others that dying is not to be feared.

Joe Dispenza is another of my favorites. He always includes accounts of people's sudden and inspirational healings in his newsletters and on his website. And I just finished reading Jeffrey Rediger's book *Cured...*

Sorry to interrupt, but we could tell you were getting carried away by your own enthusiasm, which is a good thing, but we need to point out here that most individuals who are diagnosed with incurable illnesses accept the diagnosis and go to their deaths, unhealed. And this is why we are so eager to dialogue with you. Because together we will produce a practical treatise that lays out how, even in the midst of full-blown disease, pain, and suffering, a person can choose again. They can choose life over death and love over fear.

[The next day]

Thank you for the clarification regarding the purpose of illness. I do have something else I'd like to discuss with you. Is now a good time?

Yes, we have told you before that our door is always open and our office hours are twenty-four seven.

I just got home from a session with Noa during which we discussed, among other things, the process of healing.

Yes, and...?

What she said is something I've heard before but seems to be slightly contradictory to what you've said. I just don't want to think about the possibility that something you said contradicts something she said.

We would like to ease your mind by reminding you that in the quantum, contradictions do not exist, that is, they are not significant. Neither are paradoxes or conundrums or any other word you can think of that expresses a contrast, a comparison, or a dichotomy. And that is because, as you well know by now, in the quantum all possibilities exist. We will grant that on the material plane people are routinely pronouncing one thing "right" and the other thing "wrong," hence your need to clarify this issue. Please give us the details of Noa's revelation today.

Noa said that my leukemia is my body's attempt to keep me safe, and that when the thought forms that created the illness are healed, there will no longer be any need for the illness to exist, and it will go away.

We do not see any contradiction between that and what we have said previously. Granted, we have not approached the subject from that angle, but we see it as a helpful way to view illness. Especially since we have affirmed the divine intelligence of the body, we deem it not helpful to posit a body gone awry, one that aims to annihilate or at the very least attack its inhabitant.

I have heard that said about autoimmune diseases, that is, that they're a result of the body attacking itself. It doesn't feel good to think that your own body has turned on you.

No, it's not helpful. You will find that all of our profound pronouncements regarding health and disease are based on the degree to which they are helpful in understanding and healing the disease. You will never hear us pronounce something to be outright "wrong," although we will describe things as more or less helpful.

Okay, but previously I was using the metaphor of little lost sheep to describe the manifestations of my disease. Now you're saying my body created those lost sheep to keep me safe?

Not exactly. Your physical body doesn't create anything unbidden. As ACIM reminds you, "My body is a wholly neutral thing." Just as your egoic mind creates disease manifestations, your subconscious mind, in its infinite wisdom, can also create such manifestations but with a higher purpose intended, one example of which would be to keep you safe, as mentioned previously in the little lost sheep reference. Another might be to clear your ancestral line of its prevailing fear. Another might be to assist others in their awakening. Or it might be all of the above.

I'm having a hard time accepting that my subconscious mind would do such a thing.

Yes, understood. Just because you can't accept it does not make it untrue. Your best choice would be to remember that your subconscious mind wishes nothing but the best for you.

90

Do you think this explanation applies to all forms of disease or just to cancer?

We see this explanation as valid for all illnesses. It is especially apparent in cases of cancer, and that is because cancer is a disease of accretion, characterized by the buildup of cells into structures called tumors. In your case, your body corrals the errant white blood cells into one location in the body, the lymph nodes, and keeps them from invading the rest of your beautiful organism. They are in this holding pen of sorts until you, the consciousness directing the show, learn to replace negative thoughts with stories of love and empowerment.

Thanks for that explanation. I do like to try to understand things.

I do have one more topic of discussion before we end this chapter, and it involves the idea of lifestyle changes and how to look upon them, especially since you have been asserting all along that illness isn't caused by anything physical. Why then, should people try to change their behavior and adopt healthy habits in areas such as diet and exercise? This is especially pertinent now because we are at the beginning of a new year, and there is a lot of talk about whether or not new year's resolutions are helpful. What do you think is the value in adopting healthier habits, and what enables people to make behavior changes that are long-lasting?

That is the $64,000 question, to harken back to a TV show of bygone days. It's what health coaches and doctors and psychiatrists and helpers of all stripes would like to know and be able to convey to their patients. Of course, the answer does not lie in the realm of the material. Physical enticements are short-lived.

What, then, well and truly motivates humans? It all starts with... ta da... can you guess? Yes, Dear One's already guessed it: Love of self, and that would be love coming from one's Soul Self. That is, in essence, the missing link in all the behavior change literature, the thousands of research papers which were preceded by all those millions of dollars in research funding produced by all those innumerable post docs earnestly and urgently looking for answers to the simple question: What motivates humans to change their behavior so they're healthier and thus happier? And the simple answer to the simple question is access to and engagement with the Soul Self.

You see, living in a healthy manner is the natural outcome of loving yourself and living in the quantum. A healthy lifestyle cannot be imposed from outside that realm.

True, it's a simple answer, but one that just might take a lifetime to accomplish, if Dear One here is any example. She eats in a healthy way because she loves and values her body and wants to conserve and perpetuate it. She exercises and does any other number of health practices because she wants to have the best performing vehicle on the road as possible. She wants to fulfill her mission in this lifetime and doesn't want to waste any precious time being in the repair shop. Yes, we have to confess, we are thinking of Chitty Chitty Bang Bang, and we are sure we never ever saw the movie, but we think it was about a car.

Yes, I just consulted Wikipedia, and Chitty Chitty Bang Bang was indeed a car which could fly. It was made into a really silly movie in the 1960s. I don't think I ever saw it either.

Yes, a perfect allusion. Your body is indeed like a car that can fly. You just throw it into overdrive and off you go into the wild blue. You have gradually become aware of your ability to access the quantum state. Whether you get there by jumping or via Chitty Chitty Bang Bang, the result is the same. You are in a state in which there is no doubt about who you are or what you need to do to keep yourself in tip top shape. We hope that answers your question about behavior change.

Chapter 6
What Keeps Me from Healing?

Dear One, in good and earnest faith, asks the question, "what keeps me from healing?"

We will present some ideas that came up during our morning conversations by telling some creative and interesting stories Dear One has concocted to make sure healing does not occur. We are calling them ego stories.

Before we start the prosecution of the crimes and transgressions of the ego, we would like to say a few words in its defense.

This is surprise testimony, coming from you, Pliny! Didn't I hear you say that the misguided thoughts originating from what we're calling the ego are responsible for all disease?

The ego is entitled to a fair trial, is it not? Many "thoughty" people, including Dear One here, attempt to separate their spiritual selves from their egoic selves. They see the ego as the villain and imprison it, thus making it unavailable for rehabilitation and parole. We are here to tell you that in spite of what ACIM would lead you to believe, the ego is necessary for your survival and, in fact, plays an important part in your spiritual development. Enfolding the egoic self into the spiritual self is the work of a lifetime, but work that is well worth the effort because it makes it possible for the individual to be fully human and at the same time fully godlike in a marriage that celebrates the oneness of God's creation.

That is our defense of the ego. It gets its bad-boy reputation because often the personality mistakes the ego for the true self, not the product of misguided thoughts based on prior experience. This can, and most often does, create havoc in every area of human life. The ego constructs a false front, like those storefronts in TV westerns with built-up facades which made the building look more imposing and grander. But the ego's underlying motives are benign all along. It is just trying to keep its human safe to prevent those hurtful actions and reactions such as have occurred in the past.

Okay. I accept that the ego is a necessary part of being human, and I can even go along with the idea that its motives are benign. But what about the fact that it creates such misery and suffering for humans? Do you want to present the case against the ego as well as defend it?

That's not a problem for us, as you know well our facility with both/and thinking. This is the case called Ego v. Humanity in which the ego is accused of creating disease in humans. A pretty serious charge we would say. Prior to the trial, however, I would like to round up other possible culprits.

Ah, here is the body stepping forward. Body, are you guilty of creating these health problems, willfully and without aforethought of the consequences for your hapless human? No, Body adamantly denies the accusation. We would further question whether perhaps Body thought it was by chance, by some unfortunate accident, that the illness came upon it? No, Body denies the likelihood of this proposition as well.

Other suspects, please step forward as a group to be interrogated. Unhealthy Diet, Environmental Toxins, Sedentary Lifestyle, Genetic Predisposition, and Poor Sleep Habits have all come to the front of the courtroom. What do you have to say for yourselves? Ah, just so... they are saying that although they might have been present at the scene, they did not do the crime, and thus we cannot accuse them of causality and make them do the time.

Now please call the human's Thinking Mind, also known as consciousness, but with a small c, and also called ego. Oh! Thinking Mind is declining to testify because it refuses to incriminate itself. We are not surprised, and we will tell you why that is. Over the course of the human's lifetime, the thinking mind has so well-protected itself that it is unwilling to have its fortresses broached by any type of inquiry. Now it is detecting a defect in one of its walls and knows that, indeed, soon many of its lies will pour forth. And this, Dear One, is the point in the trial at which you find yourself presently. You have broached the walls of the ego and are willing and waiting to hear the Truth, or as much of the Truth as you are capable of hearing at this point in your spiritual development.

So, the trial is still going on, and I am just beginning to understand the extent of the lies Thinking Mind has told me. Is that correct?

Precisely, Dear One, and we are eager to share the experience with you. Together, we will be recalling, retelling, and redefining the stories your ego has brought to you over the years, which have become stuck in your consciousness and solidified in your body in the form of illness. This process is without a doubt the most essential part of healing. It has been called soul integration, which does not mean that the soul is not already completely and well-integrated, but rather that the human consciously participates in the process of bringing truth to lies to create a masterpiece that reflects its true nature. This is the work of lifetimes for every spirit who ever chose to incarnate.

I am aware of at least some of the stories my Thinking Mind has told me. Shall I get on with recounting a few of them? I can't change the fact that they happened, but I can change the meaning I attach to them, right?

We are not in agreement that you cannot change events that happened in the past, since time is not operational in the quantum. But please, proceed with the stories. We think they will be entertaining as well as edifying, and as we have said, bringing them to light is therapeutic in itself.

One of the biggest issues I've been able to identify so far is my inability to express myself, as in to give my opinion if I think it might be unpopular, to defend myself if I'm feeling criticized, or to speak up when I perceive an injustice being done to someone else. As a child, I remember being shushed a lot and told "Children should be seen and not heard." I didn't come from a family of big talkers, and I wasn't a particularly gregarious child, but I remember one incident that really embarrassed me.

I might have been six or seven years old, and we had guests at the house. I can't remember who they were or why they were there. I do remember that I was talking about something when one of my parents shushed me. I remember thinking at the time that none of the adults was saying much. They certainly weren't saying anything interesting, so I figured I would help out. I still remember the shame that I felt as a result of that reprimand. I was mortified.

Mortified? Interesting word choice. Dear One was a very sensitive child, and while we will admit that this incident may not be as dire as other more extreme examples of physical and emotional abuse that children experience, it was pivotal for her and left an emotional scar, as evidenced by the fact that she remembers it seventy years later. Dear One learned that it is not safe to voice her opinions and feelings, that it's better to say nothing to avoid potential criticism or disapproval. Dear One's voice was effectively shut off as a result of that seemingly mild rebuke. Is it any wonder that disease is manifesting now mainly in her neck and throat area? We think not.

Situations which call for me to speak up, either in self-defense or even just to give information, have always been challenging for me. I have a pathological fear of public speaking. My throat constricts, and my voice gets raspy when I have to speak to groups of any more than about twelve people. Twelve seems to be the upper threshold of my comfort limit. Years ago, I joined a Toastmasters group in an effort to overcome the problem, but I was never able to conquer my anxiety. I even volunteered to chair a large all-staff weekly meeting at the hospital where I was working. It was a total disaster; at least, that's how I remember it.

May we interject a comment here? Yes, you saw it as a total disaster, but many others did not. They saw a courageous woman dealing with one of her greatest fears. How inspiring must that have been for them, we ask you. Can you tell us how this story has changed over the years?

The fact that I'm writing this very personal tell-all book is one indication that things have changed. I'm also anticipating becoming comfortable with speaking engagements because I'm going to need to do that to publicize this book. I even had a crazy idea that I would have a life-size cardboard standup Pliny replica made. I would take it to speaking engagements so I would always remember that you, Pliny, are always with me. Do you like that idea?

Yes, we are thrilled to be on stage with you. But how are you going to get us into the car? Are we foldable?

Yes, well you always tell me to be flexible, right?

Ah hahaha.

Here's another mind movie you have created that relates to the topic at hand. We're seeing you as a whiney, fussy baby, perhaps eighteen months old. You are in your playpen in the living room, and you want mightily to get out. Your creativity is being purposely thwarted by that big mean person called Mommy. And to add insult to injury, she comes into the room from the kitchen and admonishes you for making a fuss. You're like: "What? I'm supposed to stay in this jail and not complain?"

And, dear little Joy, we would agree that it makes no sense whatsoever. If you're unhappy, you should shout it from the rooftops. This was the beginning of the suffocation of Joy which is now manifesting as enlarged tonsils and other lymph nodes in the neck. But little Joy was a quick learner, and she learned that making a fuss did not get her what she wanted, which was love and attention from Mommy. And she generalized that to all people and relationships. Don't make a fuss, go along with the program, and on the way there, please as many people as possible. Maybe then they will love you.

I'm aware that my mother's upbringing had a profound effect on her psyche, and that she was just doing what came naturally, that is, passing along her dysfunction to me.

Yes, little Joy learned from Mommy that she was nothing special. You see, Mommy grew up on a farm in Ohio during the Great Depression. Life was hard, and there wasn't enough food or love to go around. There were many cats on that farm, none of which was really special. They caught the rats and mice but were all expendable. It certainly wouldn't make sense to lavish love and attention on a farm cat. Little

Joy learned at eighteen months to feel like one of those farm cats. She learned that her best bet would be to get really good at catching rats and mice because there were no rewards for being special.

[The next day]

I'm in the process of preparing for a housewarming party which I'm having here in a few days. I feel like a hamster scurrying on the wheel in my cage. I know this is an old story, one I learned as a child. I can remember my mother preparing for a party and being absolutely wigged out at the thought of guests coming to the house. Everything must be perfect. Oof, I'm getting a tummy ache just thinking about it.

Dear One is a very quick learner. Like a sponge, we would say. By eighteen months, she had mastered the art of tuning into Mommy's energy to determine how to feel. And how Mommy felt was never—well, hardly ever—good. There was always a cloud of free-floating anxiety around Mommy. And sometimes, the anxiety was attached to something specific, such as the dinner party Dear One has described. Mommy's life on the farm in the Depression was precarious, characterized by lack and uncertainty, a situation made doubly difficult by the necessity to deny the fact. Yes, you had to cover up the deprivation and put on a good front for the benefit of the world and specifically the neighbors. Such is Dear One's inheritance. Luckily, thanks to the grace of God, it is not her legacy. She has received the great gift of expanded awareness, which she has shared with her daughter and anyone else who will listen. Ah hahaha!

Dear One, we feel you tugging on the reins. Can you please leave off doing that?

Yes, you're right. It's just that I have so many theories and stories about Mommy's dysfunctionality.

We are wanting to come through with some new material regarding Mommy rather than rehashing your old theories. Mommy and her father, known to you as Grandpa, had a very intense karmic relationship. And the unfoldment of that relationship was primary in Mommy's life. Naturally, Grandma was jealous of this close connection because Grandpa so obviously adored Mommy. Hence Mommy's lifelong tendency toward jealousy, caused by an unconscious need to resolve that conflict with her mother.

We hope you are finding this discussion edifying. We think it's helpful to be aware of the line of ego stories that have been passed to you generationally. This awareness can assist you not only in feeling compassion for your family members, but also in pointing out the opportunity that you now have to heal your lineage. Since time is not a factor in the quantum, the hurts and wounds of your great-grandmother are as available and able to be brought up for healing as those of your mother and your daughter. We are mentioning female relatives only since these egoic themes tend to be gender related. Here again, awareness is the prerequisite for healing.

[The next day]

I got from our conversation yesterday that it's important to come from an authentic place in order to bring about healing of disease. Did I get that right?

Yes, it's not only important, but it's also absolutely necessary!

Sometimes I feel that I've been coming from an inauthentic place my whole life. And by that, I mean pretending to feel things I don't feel and doing things I don't want to do all in an effort to be loved. You know, all that stuff stemming from my childhood.

Yes, we are well aware, but just to summarize, the personality that is Joy grew up in a family that didn't appreciate her preciousness. She was deemed a nuisance if she asserted herself, and she grew up thinking that in order to be loved, she needed to avoid making a fuss, making noise, or saying what she really felt. She concluded that her value, nay, her very life, depended on working hard and producing results since there was absolutely no value placed on her "beingness," that is her innate lovability. No adult ever affirmed that consistently for her. The only exception she can think of right now might have been her violin teacher, Mr. Randall, whom she adored, and who affirmed her value during her weekly violin lessons no matter how good, bad, or mediocre her playing was.

Now I'm wondering if my hearing loss, which has been diagnosed as mild to moderate depending on which ear and which frequency, is connected in any way to an ego story. Perhaps to the unworthiness story?

Brava, Dear One! We're glad you're wondering about that because, as we've said before, all disease is related in some way to your misperceptions and faulty egoic conclusions. Now you are remembering your Great-Uncle Lawrence who had profound hearing loss and was a totally repulsive and repugnant character. That's how little Joy saw him, admit it!

Yes, he was pretty distasteful.

Not only that, but he also liked to tickle little Joy, and he did it with hard fingers. Yes, he did. And little Joy felt helpless to fend him off. Furthermore, no adults came to her rescue.

Do you think that it's possible this abuse might have something to do with Joy's hearing problems now?

I'm having trouble connecting the dots. Why would my current hearing problems have anything to do with Uncle Lawrence?

You might want to marinate in the question. The answer will come forth; perhaps not right away, but in rereading or in the editing process. Here's just a hint: Do you think it might relate to self-worth? Might Joy have created a false self based on what she perceived as other people's perception of her? Really, not such a brilliant conclusion because everything you have thus far identified as a problem in your life is in some way related to self-worth.

Thank you, Pliny. I'll put that in my big glass marination bowl for twenty-four hours. That should tenderize it enough so I can chew on it.

[The next day]

Initially, I had a hard time connecting something so seemingly trivial as tickling with something as serious as hearing loss. I see now, though, that as a child I was helpless to stop the abuse, and the fact that adults didn't step in to protect me confirmed my opinion of myself as insignificant and unimportant.

Another thought occurred to me while I was marinating. Uncle Lawrence might have abused my mother in the same way, possibly even more seriously because he was around her more when she was a child.

Well, good marinating, Dear One! Although we're not the ones to confirm or deny the possibility of Uncle Lawrence's more serious abuse of your mother, we would say this is a very fruitful line of inquiry. Humans have recently become aware of their ability to do ancestral healing. It involves awakened souls assisting other souls in their lineage to clean up their karma, which consists of the consequences of thoughts and actions throughout lifetimes on the physical plane. It is a very productive endeavor because the extent to which this happens affects the extent of the forward progress humanity can make during the coming epoch. We are pleased to see you exercising your abilities in this area.

Thanks for your encouragement, but I've got another ego story I've just begun to deal with that I'd like to talk about. I think of it as guilt, or maybe it's shame. Whatever it is, it feels very uncomfortable.

Could it be that you find it so uncomfortable that you've been unwilling to even take it out of the box to look at it? Rather than a box, we're seeing a sort of bottom-of-the-sea pirate's chest, just waiting to be opened and the hidden treasure revealed. Please, give us an example of how this ego story plays out in your life.

Last week I got a COVID booster shot, and I didn't feel well for a few days afterward. I saw clearly how I abuse myself when I'm sick. I impose what I imagine are other people's expectations on my behavior which makes it difficult to rest and recuperate. I feel that I should be up and about, accomplishing things as usual. It feels like an old pattern of not feeling well, not doing something or going somewhere, and then making excuses for not doing it and feeling guilty about it.

Yes, we're glad you noticed that. Guilt serves no one. Your state of mind should be your only focus. To paraphrase Abraham, the entity channeled by Esther Hicks, getting to the next better-feeling thought is your only job. Success might come in small increments, such as going from a feeling of guilt, which is low on the vibrational scale, to one slightly higher, anger for instance. Are you following us here? We're sensing that you are pulling on the reins again. Please leave off doing that, lest we have to beat you about the head and shoulders. Ah hahaha. That's a joke. We would never do that.

Oh, I just got a hit of your merriment. You do love to laugh, don't you?

Yes, and we know you to be one who delights in a humorous situation. We are seriously concerned for those who don't partake in the deliciousness. What more serious thoughts have been clouding your otherwise sunny horizon?

Where shall I start? I'm concerned I may be losing my mind. You know, going the route of my mother's neighbor Marge. As I recall, Marge had developed some very advanced spiritual ideas during her lifetime but had difficulty with societal expectations. She would make outrageous statements and do upsetting things like go to church with her clothes half on, zippers unzipped, hair askew. It was distressing for the neighbors.

We know the spirit that was Marge. She was greeted with much fanfare when she arrived on this side. By the way, there are no sides. She led a courageous and adventurous life.

Yes, we are happy to confirm that you are losing your mind, or rather losing your thinking mind, we should say. You are in the process of "forgiving the world all you thought it was," as it is so aptly put in ACIM.

You see, forgiveness doesn't apply only to people, it applies also to false thoughts and perceptions that do not serve you. And believe you us, you have many of them. This latest episode of illness showed you how you let those false ideas of other peoples' expectations cause discomfort in you. And do you want to feel guilty? NO! It's one of the more unpalatable feelings on your feelings menu.

Here is a good place to point out that trust is an important part, nay, an essential part of the process of awakening.

Trust that although you are losing your so-called mind, it is for the best and will be accompanied by an upgrade to your electrical system. Trust that the water in the lake will keep you afloat. Trust beyond that voracious need of yours to understand intellectually.

[The next day]

Do you think it's necessary to forgive in order to heal?

A consciousness that's clouded by unforgiving thoughts is not one that's likely to be healed. We used the word likely because you do know, and we know you know, that the quantum includes all possibilities. Now, if you were to ask us about the probability of healing for a mean, unforgiving curmudgeon, we would say, "We don't know, but we are affirming a certain percentage of healing possibility for that unforgiving curmudgeon."

While we're on the topic of forgiveness and relationships, I've had something on my mind that I've been reluctant to talk about.

As your teacher Noa reminds you, "There are no secrets in the quantum, and just because the so-called secret thoughts are not voiced by you in the physical does not mean that they're unknown to the All That Is." The beans have already been spilled, Dear One. You may proceed to soak them and cook them. May we suggest your delicious chili recipe?

I'm feeling confused and uncertain about my relationship with my boyfriend.

Yes, we know exactly that feeling because we can put ourselves in your emotional shoes. But why don't you outline for us as precisely as you can the reasons for your upset?

When we're together I get pulled out of my emotional center, my place of peace, my Soul Self, you might call it. Why is it that I get triggered so consistently and revert to my ego self so quickly?

May we suggest that there's some healing to be done somewhere in the vicinity? Can you guess where?

Yes, well it feels like childhood stuff. And my boyfriend has so many of the annoying characteristics of my mother. Could it be unresolved stuff involving my mother?

"La la, la. Hum, hum hum." It's your mother humming a tuneless and annoying little ditty while standing in front of the stove doing what she calls cooking. Meanwhile, you are about to blow a gasket because you have something to say and she's off in her cloud of distraction. Your sky is falling, and you can't get her attention. The only possible explanation is that you're not worthy of it. Yes, attention from the mother was something Dear One did not get enough of as a child. And as an adult, although she always downplays her need for center stage, the attention deficit is still there in the form of a hole in her concept of self. It is a hole that cannot be filled in by anyone other than her precious self.

We're bringing up the example from Dear One's childhood because the boyfriend tends to do the same thing, that is, downplay her strong emotions and ignore the fact that she has symptoms related to her illness.

You're right. He likes to tell me that I don't show any outward signs of being sick, I think in an attempt to be reassuring. But that invalidates some of my strong negative emotions such as fear. He's wanting to sweep those nasty feelings under the rug rather than let me bring them out and investigate them. He's not up for investigating them together, certainly.

Correct. His primary ego need is to keep the status quo, to keep the relationship boat from rocking. He doesn't want to

*lose you to death and is not ready or willing to entertain
that possibility. Quantum jumping is what's called for here.
Just jump out of that silly boat into the quantum consciousness we've been talking about. We feel your doubt that this
would be possible in this situation, and we would like to
remind you that the quantum is the realm of infinite
variation where everything is possible.*

Yes, but the quantum realm also involves probability, and the
probability of me being able to change things in our relationship is
nil.

*Aha! Caught you in a lie. That is absolutely not true. You
are much more powerful than you think in this and every
other situation. Do you want to leave this relationship just
as you've left every other relationship in your long life?*

No, I don't want to do that. We love each other, and there's a lot
that's good in our relationship. But can you give me any advice
about how to stay in my Soul Self and not get triggered?

*Talk. Real, authentic talk coming from your expanded self.
He won't understand much of what you say but will connect
to the emotional vibration of your speech. If you speak from
that deep well of love for him, he will respond in kind, and
you will both feel heard and understood. Now, doesn't it feel
better to be loved and loving rather than judgmental?*

Yes, thank you. Since we were talking about my need for attention,
I'd like to bring up an insight I had recently about why I have not
healed my illness yet. But first, let me ask: Do you think it's true
that some part of me must perceive some benefit in being sick, or
otherwise I would heal?

*We are thinking that this is a very simplistic analysis of a
very complex subject, but in general, we would confirm its
validity. And where is it that you'd like to go with this line
of questioning?*

Well, right before I went to bed the other night, I asked my subconscious to reveal to me any perceived but unrecognized benefit I might derive from being sick. My subconscious told me that it feels the illness gets me the attention I want. Also, when I was a child, being sick got me out of things I didn't want to do, things such as gym class, taking a math test, even going to the dreaded swimming lesson. It goes back as far as my adolescence.

Oh, it goes back even further than that, Dear One. These feelings have circulated in your subconscious your entire life and even in prior lives as well. The key to dealing with them is NOT uprooting them and throwing them on the compost heap, but rather dissolving them with your consciousness and then reabsorbing the particles back into your energetic system.

Okay. Here's another ego story I learned early on: What other people think of me is more important than what I think of me.

We will begin our comments on that topic with a little platitude:

To thine own self be true,

Really ain't nothin' else to do.

We are noticing that you're afraid we'll embarrass ourselves and yourself as well. We would like to proclaim, loudly and from the rooftops, that it doesn't matter to us if we embarrass ourselves or not because we're not concerned about how others see us.

Frankly, we don't give a rip, and neither should you. You've cared a lot during this lifetime about how other people see you. And has that habit of mind led to any of the following:

- *More fun?*
- *More creative success?*
- *More enjoyment of life?*

- *More je ne sais quoi?*

No, we thought not. What we're trying to get across is this: Go ahead, embarrass yourself. Get it over with, and you'll feel much better.

[The next day]

We're feeling very frisky this morning, as you can tell. Irreverent, even. Yes, it's okay to be irreverent toward things to which no reverence is due, such as some, if not all, of societal norms and prohibitions. Children who have not yet been socialized or otherwise completely squelched by parental or societal influences are great examples for us to follow. And we would urge you to be as childlike as possible.

We feel you have had a heaviness hanging about your head and shoulders that is not really consistent with child's play. It has been there for a while now and has come in response to your focused attention on your illness. We would prefer to see you laughing. Get out of Camp Swampy and lighten up. You see, it is a choice. Choose to be joyous. Do only those things that bring you joy.

Nothing brings me much joy lately except moments in meditation when I transcend the physical world.

And we would respectfully reply RUBBISH! You are a prime enjoyer of the physical senses, and you can't tell us otherwise. We know you intimately. We have purposely installed in you a new operating system so that you can return to heaven on Earth. Don't waste your time anywhere else. You can have your feet firmly planted on terra firma and still be 100 percent connected to the heavens. In fact, this is not only advisable, but also it's required if you want to be healthy. Any other state is damaging to the body. You are doing marvelously well, by the way, in the adjustment to the new operating system. Just a little tweaking, and we think we've got it.

Tweak away!

[The next day]

Here's another ego story: I must be perfect. What profound insights or earth-shattering pronouncements do you have to make about this one?

Now we've got to be profound or earth-shattering on demand?

And speaking of applying the pressure, which we just were, you, Dear One, have been applying the pressure to yourself for many years. And where has it gotten you? In hot water, we would say. And now that you have your new Instant Pot, you can pressurize yourself in no time flat and come out fork tender. Yes, we jest with you again, but the above analogies are not far from the truth.

We do not recommend pressurizing yourself, but we do understand why the personality that is Joy does that to herself. It is a question of habituation. And we are feeling the energy in the second-grade classroom of the beautiful and blonde Mrs. Edna Armstrong. Loudly, she is saying, "round, round, ready, write," an incantation that precedes a cursive handwriting exercise in the Palmer Method of penmanship. Little eight-year-old Joy is trying so hard to make her left-handed letters come out correctly. They don't look like those of the other children, but they must be perfect so that Mrs. Armstrong will approve and shower little Joy with love, something which she feels she's painfully lacking. Yes, of course little Joy feels the pressure. Her very survival depends on perfection! That explains her tendency to pressurize herself now. And now that we understand that and feel those second-grade feelings of desperate yearning and unrealized hope, it is time to lay that perfection thing to rest.

Thank you, I *so* totally agree! I just wanted to discuss a variation on the perfection theme, that is the need to look good, no matter what.

Yes, Dear One was duly indoctrinated with the "If you look good, you ARE good" school of thought by Mommy, who did, indeed, look very good. She continued to look good almost until the day she died. She was a knockout at ninety and hadn't lost much ground at 101. She was starting to fade, but only slightly, at age 102 when she finally transitioned.

As a young woman, Mommy received much attention and approval because of her good looks. She concluded that appearance was primary, and even if all else went to hell, her good looks would sustain her. She, in fact, developed some narcissistic tendencies. It was not easy being the less-than-beautiful daughter of the star that was Mommy, and Dear One grew up knowing that she would never measure up in the looks department.

Growing up in the 1950s, she didn't hear too much about developing inner resources. Character development consisted of doing things outside one's comfort zone in order to build strength and determination, such as playing competitive sports like soccer and volleyball, activities which Dear One, of course, loathed.

[The next day]

This morning I woke up knowing that I still have more work to do in the self-love department, specifically loving my appearance despite the ever-growing lymph nodes under my chin causing swelling on the sides of my face. How can I love a face such as this, I ask you?

Please realize that you have called forth this situation at this time in order for it to be healed. As we have said many times before, your lymph nodes are your creation. That is, they have materialized as a result of thoughts—mostly conscious thoughts we would add—that are wanting to be recognized and gathered in and incorporated into your awareness.

What is called for here is nothing more or less than total trust in the workings of the Universe, beyond the need to understand why things are unfolding as they are and what the outcome may be. We are describing a relaxation into the certainty that all is well, and a surrender to the experience that you are now—always have been, and always will be— safe in the care of the All That Is. If that doesn't give you some comfort, we don't know what will.

That does give me comfort, but I still have so many stories connected with my not-good-enough appearance. Would it help me to replay them and then look in the mirror and bring up loving, accepting feelings toward myself and my current chipmunk appearance?

Yes, good plan. And who doesn't love a chipmunk? They are so cute and perky! Ah hahaha. We are glad to see you lightening up a bit. That in itself is healing.

I was thinking…

Uh-oh.

Just one more little ego story I'd like to get your take on. It's about my habit of criticizing myself about my use of time. Yesterday I spent my day doing only what I wanted to, which was reading and napping. And I told myself I had an unproductive day.

Yes, you did. And we would say unproductive by whose standards? Some very stern taskmaster, we would imagine. We think she might have a pencil sticking out of the bun atop her head. Please, stop this destructive and habitual way of thinking immediately. Your job, and your ONLY job we might add, is to express as fully as possible the soul we know and love as Dear One.

You are clearing out years of detritus (we love it when we can use that word) from your psyche. What comes to mind is the recent and unfortunate collapse of a condominium in Florida due to structural degradation. Likewise, the infrastructure of your psyche has collapsed in a very dramatic and resounding manner. It was composed of the mostly untrue stories and unconscious conditioning that created a very misleading picture of who you were. Now you are faced with the cleanup, a herculean task, but one that you don't have to undertake alone. You may use your psychic telephone and call up the Angelic Debris Removal and Salvage Team. They will come to the rescue. By the way, they may appear to be angelic, but don't let that fool you. They are also mighty and powerful and more than able to get the job done. We don't want to be alarmists, but there may be other wings of the structure that are degraded and in danger of collapse. Please call for help immediately.

Good advice, Pliny. I will call as soon as we're done talking.

Actually, no need to call. They are already on the job as we speak. The collapse of your ego sense of self has created some cognitive discontinuity which will take time and assistance to clean up. Please be patient with yourself as the cleanup proceeds. Take time for leisure activities such as reading and napping and do only those activities which reward you with pleasure molecules.

Chapter 7
Taxes, Death, and Doctors

Are we ready for this glorious, upbeat, and triumphal chapter Dear One has decided to call Taxes, Death, and Doctors?

Yes, I'm ready and even eager to hear what you have to say on the subject.

Let us clarify that taxes, death, and doctors are all very distinct subjects, and not really related, as your chapter title implies. And even though we have said that all is one in the quantum, we judge that it is less than helpful to discuss them as if they were the same (or even related) topics.

Taxes are in the category of something that exists solely on the material plane, a fact of life for many humans. Taxes are determined, regulated, and administered by the regime in power at a given moment in time on the social/political/ economic material-world landscape. It has been thus ever since humans emerged from caves, hence the phrase "death and taxes" indicating inevitability and the futility of resistance.

We know that humans enjoy discussing and protesting what they judge as misuse of tax moneys, and some are called to take action to correct what they see as injustices in the existing system. And to those brave activists, we say Bravo! Brava! Carry on, but check yourself for righteous anger or indignation, please. Take action, by all means, but make sure it is action based on love for humankind and your desire to better things for everyone. In other words, please examine what is motivating you to act and make sure those motivations are pure and they are pointing to the highest and best outcome. If they are based on ego stories or mind movies you have made from personal injustices experienced in the past, we suggest you sit down and meditate and ask for forgiveness and guidance. Basically, we are asking you to jump into the quantum before proceeding with resistance or civil disobedience.

By the way, we noticed that we just laid out a plan for any type of enlightened action, not restricted to political action or just tax-related matters. We have discussed this previously, but it is well worth repeating since humans are currently perceiving an increase in strife and violence on the planet and finding no good solutions on the material level. This level of dysfunction has disheartened many, and some are finding it difficult to remain connected to their Soul Selves. To those individuals, we would say, "Look to your heart because your heart is pointing the way to the solution." Your heart will tell you that in your many and varied lifetimes, you've been the perpetrator as well as the victim, and all seeming evil in the world is but a cry for love. When more of humanity incorporates this into their consciousness, peace and love will replace strife and hate.

Thank you, Pliny. That's so encouraging, even though it seems like that time might be a long way off.

Here we would add that even if humanity can't get it together in time to avoid extinction, consciousness will abide, and other life forms will emerge in time.

Wow, thanks for that information! I'm not sure why, but I find that oddly comforting.

[The next day]

Since this chapter includes the topic of taxes, can I recount my tax-related story for the benefit of our dear readers?

Yes, yes. Please recount. We judge it will be helpful for some.

This past spring I was really worried, and I mean REALLY worried, that I would have to pay a lot in taxes. The previous year, I had purchased a new and expensive (for me) townhome. I don't have any federal tax withheld from my retirement income, and I wasn't sure where the money would come from to pay the income tax that year. It took me several weeks to gather the information to send to my accountant, during which time I was getting more and more upset.

We are aware that the personality that is Joy is much disturbed by income taxes preparation. We do have some reassurance for the frightened child that is Joy.

First and foremost, please know the Internal Revenue Service is not God, though it is sometimes seen as a punishing god in your society. Secondly, your financial insecurities arise from the mistaken notion that you are separate from your fellow humans and from God. If you could get but a whiff of the magnitude of this misperception, it would go a long way to ease your fears. You are not alone and never have been. You can ask for help and support from your friends, and you can ask the same from God, who loves you beyond measure.

Has there ever been a time when Joy's needs have not been met by a benevolent Universe? Sometimes, your fear has blinded you to the fact that, indeed, Joy has always been taken care of. So you may carry on with your dithering and fear creation OR you may calmly and assuredly get the job done. File the return, pay the tax if needs be, and move on with your abundant life. Time to choose. "More suffering, please" or "Enough of suffering, thank you."

Thank you, Pliny. When I take the fear out of the equation, it all seems so much more manageable. And, it turned out I owed no tax whatsoever! All that worry was for nothing.

We are happy to report that the same principle applies to death. No matter how many times we discarnates tell you there is no death, just a transfer of energy from the physical to the quantum, you don't really believe us. This accounts for all the fear and loathing humans have surrounding the subject. Think of how the material world would change if humans learned not to fear death.

It's hard for me even to imagine, Pliny. Tell me how that would be.

Deaths will be celebrated much as birthdays are now. Farewell parties will be planned in advance of the death and families and friends will celebrate the person's life and their return to the nonphysical. Sure, survivors will still grieve for the loss of the deceased's physical presence, but they will be reassured by the knowledge that their loved one's spirit is still very much alive, yet just moved on to another form of consciousness. Communication with deceased persons will be frequent and common because fear has been removed from the equation. Humans will look forward to hearing from their dearly departed and will be further comforted by this communication, knowing that the spirit of the deceased is alive and well, doing whatever needed to be done in the quantum, perhaps reviewing the previous life for ideas for improvement for the next time on the merry-go-round. Souls are not just twiddling their thumbs between lives, you know.

It is most unfortunate that humans hold this horror of death. It is paralyzing, mortifying, and totally unnecessary. Even though Dear One has spent years researching accounts of what happens to souls after death, she still remains partially unconvinced about the glory that is death. Perhaps this is so in part because pain and suffering often attend the end of life. This, too, is a choice, however, and by that we mean it doesn't have to be that way.

I do believe strongly my spirit will never die, so I'm not sure why I'm so hesitant to embrace death more fully. Perhaps it's all the negative attention it gets in society. There is such doom and gloom surrounding the subject.

Your distrust of death is directly related to your lack of trust in God and the workings of the Universe. Your trust is situational, shaky at best. Here's an illustration of how you're feeling: You're crossing a hanging bridge spanning a very deep and wide chasm. You're holding onto the handrails that run along the sides, but many of the wooden slats on the walkway are missing or broken. Sometimes your foot goes through a weakened slat and only your grip on the handrails keeps you from plunging through the bridge to your death on the rocks below.

I get the picture.

In the face of these seemingly dangerous circumstances, there's a place in you that knows you only need fly to the other side to avoid tragedy, yet somehow you are unable to do it. You just can't get liftoff.

Ahem... don't even think about interrupting here. We're on a roll.

We would like to prescribe daily practice of the levitation meditation, which was given to you by your teacher, Noa. This will surprise, amaze, and delight you because after some practice you will be successful in levitating. This will be your evidence that all that has been told to you about the quantum realm is true. You are now at a stage where you have cleaned out enough of the gunk (lies) that you are ready to levitate. It will be a wonderful, joyous practice and will serve to affirm what you knew as a child but have since forgotten, that you can, indeed, fly.

Okay, I would dearly love that, and I don't think I'm being "spiritually materialistic" either.

Dear One once read something by a very learned Buddhist scholar warning about the dangers of spiritual materialism which was defined as placing value on the attainment of paranormal powers. Ever since, she has taken great pains to question herself in that regard in an effort to avoid it. Spiritual materialism is nothing more or less than the ego's attempt to usurp the experience of the quantum. We wouldn't worry too much about being called that because, as you know, we don't advise worrying about much of anything.

Do you know the reference to looking on the bright side of death? It was in the song "Always Look on the Bright Side of Life" from the movie *Monty Python's Life of Brian*.

Yes, and looking on the bright side of death is exactly what we are suggesting here. We are also suggesting that Dear Readers watch (or re-watch) the film. It was fun, very silly, and thus conducive to good health.

Back to the subject at hand, which is death. Dear One has read many, many books on the subject. Can you tell us why you've had this lifelong fascination with death?

Hmm, that sounds kind of morbid, and maybe it is. But here's the reason: I've had the strong feeling that in a previous life, death took me by surprise. I wasn't prepared for it, and I had a very difficult time accepting it. I remember having the thought that in the next lifetime, I would be prepared. I don't remember who I was when I was thinking that thought, but I know it came from me. So, I've read widely on the subject this lifetime. Most of what is written on life after death and reincarnation is from a metaphysical standpoint and written by mediums or people who have had near-death experiences because there just isn't much scientifically documented data on the topic; that is, once dead, people usually stay dead.

Raymond Moody took a more scientific approach, however, and made it his life's work to chronicle the stories of near-death experiences, looking for similarities and differences. I also loved Michael Newton's books about what happens to souls *between* lives. Newton was a psychiatrist who did past-life regressions using hypnosis. He noticed many of his patients were recounting details of what seemed to be the period between lives, that is, after they had completed one life and were in the process of planning another. Their stories contained many common features, increasing the likelihood that there is, indeed, a period of rest and review between lives. It was fascinating, and you're right, there's no thumb twiddling being done.

[The next day]

Dear One seems a bit agitated today. Can you tell us the reason for this disturbance in your energy field?

I have a doctor's appointment this afternoon and am feeling anxious about the outcome. I'd love to have your help in staying out of fear and open to love.

Yes, we always have been and always will be at your side. Did you feel the pink color wash we just poured over you?

Yes, I felt it around my heart.

> *We will use the pink-color-wash technique to reassure you of our presence. Even when the nurse puts the dreaded blood pressure cuff on your arm and starts pumping it up and you are tempted to go into your familiar panic reaction, don't. Just stop and feel our presence. Hypertension is nothing more than an indicator of a shut-down heart. But you knew that because it was told to you by your teacher, Noa. When you are in your expanded consciousness state, you have not a care whether a blood pressure reading is high or low or somewhere in between. It matters not a whit. It is merely an indicator of the level of fear you are experiencing in your body at that one brief moment in time.*

They even have a name for it, my hyperreactivity I mean. It's called the white coat syndrome, and it describes exactly what happens when a person in a white medical coat comes at me with a blood pressure cuff. I let fear hijack my well-being.

> *Yes, you do, and you have done so all these many years. It's time to stop letting anyone or anything rob you of your well-being. And please remember that the impulse for love trumps the impulse for fear whenever one is in the quantum state. Also, it matters not a whit what numbers they write down on those official-looking medical records, be they paper or electronic. They can come and go in the twinkling of an eye, but not so you, Dear One. You are eternal.*

That reminds me of a scene from my elementary school days. Our teacher was trying to control our unruly classroom, telling us that our bad behavior would go on our permanent records. I took that to mean that it would follow us throughout our school years, never to be expunged by any type or amount of good behavior, a sort of temporal version of the Akashic records.

Yes, and second-grade Joy believed that. The fact that it was said by the beautiful and much-esteemed Mrs. Edna Armstrong made it even more official AND terrifying. Even as an adult, Joy still believes that whenever she behaves badly, it goes on her permanent record. In a way, she's right about that because it's the fear created by the belief in the negative mark on her permanent record that causes the problem. The fear gets encoded in her DNA and the disease process begins.

We have already discussed the emerging field of epigenetics and how it is changing scientific thinking about the role of genes in the creation of disease. Epigenetics blasts to smithereens the idea of a genetic permanent record, by showing that genes don't by themselves determine if or when they will be expressed in the human body. Instead, the environment within and around the body determines its state of health or disease. I was really happy when I read about epigenetics. It really is a game-changer.

Not so fast! We are glad you understand that now, but it has not always been so. Just like everyone else, you have been highly conditioned by your environment. You started building an elaborate facade, a fake self, when you were very young. Even now, as an adult, you make every effort to look and act "normal," but your body belies you whenever a white-coated person takes your blood pressure. Your body reveals how scared you really are. It tells the truth, even in the face of all the lies you have learned to tell to keep yourself safe. It tells you that you still have work to do in this area even though you say you're fully onboard the epigenetics train.

I can't deny that, but it seems that my body is the hero here. She's the whistleblower. She cannot tell a lie and is willing to risk her life to tell the truth. What courage! Not only that, but she is also showing the way for others, urging them to expose their life-zapping stories and all those other fabrications that keep them from healing.

That is true, Dear One, but you needn't concern yourself with the fabrications of others. You have plenty of your own to attend to. And we don't mean to be mean here. We're just affirming the need to stay in your own yard rather than jumping the fence as you are prone to do. Even though all are one in the quantum, you are given just one personality and one body for dealing with each lifetime in the physical. Any attempt to correct others should be avoided, except, perhaps, in the case of small children or unruly dogs. We would, however, like to congratulate you on realizing that your body has been your savior here (insert drawing of clapping hands) even as your thinking brain would have cast it as villain.

Thank you for that acknowledgment. I realize that the relationship between my thinking mind and my body has completely changed. I now regard my body with awe and gratitude. I am in awe of its complexity and perfection, and I am grateful for its courage in standing up for me.

[The next day]

Now, please relate the miraculous occurrence at your doctor's appointment yesterday.

I thought you'd never ask. I'm so excited about this. To me, it's validation of what you've been saying all along, not that I didn't believe you before, of course. Before the nurse took my blood pressure, I evoked your healing presence and felt the pink color wash that you prescribed pour over me. I immediately felt that "heart bloom." I don't know what else to call it, but I'm sure you know what I mean.

I was able to maintain the feeling during the time the machine was squeezing my arm and making its nasty little clicking sounds. And voilà, nearly normal blood pressure for the first time in a medical setting in probably forty years. When I told the nurse about my heart opening trick I saw a sort of flatness in her eyes, and in a flash, my empath self realized that her heart was shut down and she saw herself as separate from her cancer patients, something that was necessary for her to feel safe. So I silently blessed her for the work she was doing, even in the face of all that fear. How courageous of her.

Which brings us to our next profound pronouncement, which is mainly for the benefit of our Dear Readers since Dear One is already well aware of it.

Ready for it?

Medical establishments are generally not safe places for human habitation, mainly because they are filled with fearful spirits and live humans with closed hearts. Of course, this is not true for every human in every medical establishment, but we would urge discernment on the part of would-be patients. Check the energy of your doctor's office. You can do this via a remote energy scan, on the phone with administrative personnel, or in a preliminary visit to the actual office. How does it feel in there? If it does not feel good, check your own heart to make sure it is open and you are not feeling your own fear. Do not stop your search until you find an office and a doctor that resonates with your own frequency. We know there is someone out there who can fill that prescription.

Yes, I am well aware of that in principle but have found it very difficult to put into practice. I can think of only one primary care doctor I've had personally who I felt had an open heart. Also, under some emergency situations, one doesn't have time to go around sensing energy.

Dear One is right again, but we would like to point out that it doesn't take any time to sense energy. It is instantaneous in every circumstance if one is open to receiving and believing the feedback. In emergency situations where medical attention is required immediately, the open heart of the patient can easily transform the energy of the whole medical team. It is truly infectious, in a good way, that is. The patient must merely be in the quantum, emanating love, and everyone in the vicinity will be healed.

Easy to say, Pliny, but not easy to do, especially when one is in pain or undergoing some kind of medical procedure.

That is why practice is so essential. Practice being in the present generous moment, as it has been called, which is the only place where healing takes place. Practice feeling the next best feeling when you are presented with challenges. Practice your meditation so you can reconnect to your Soul Self and remember your self-worth. How do you get to the quantum world? Practice, practice, practice!

Chapter 8
Quantum Jumping

Pliny, you've talked so much about the need for quantum jumping. I understand the why but I'm less clear on the how. Can you expand on what you've already said?

Yes, and here is where our prior human incarnations will aid us greatly. We clearly recall what it was like to be in a body, and at times it was most uncomfortable, as if our brains were stuck in reverse. We remember repeating self-sabotaging negative thoughts which resulted in unhappy outcomes which further reinforced our negative expectations. Picture a dog chasing his tail or—we like this one better—driving down the road looking only in the rearview mirror. And by that we mean repeating past unhappy experiences and expecting it to get you to a happier place in the future. Please know that we do commiserate with you regarding the human condition, and we so totally understand why you often wind up in places you had no intention of going.

As a matter of fact, I woke up this morning feeling sort of down, that is, not at all rarin' to go.

128

We noticed that and we want to assure you that it's not necessary to be rarin' to go all the time. What's advisable is that you be charitable toward yourself and totally accepting of whatever state of mind you're in at the moment, knowing that this too shall pass. Please do not make those negative feelings yet another reason to heap shame upon yourself. Here we want to emphasize the importance of not denying unpleasant feelings, you know, those such as fear, rage, and jealousy. These unpleasant feelings just want to be acknowledged before you can move on to better-feeling emotions.

My teacher, Noa, reminded me the other day of the importance of feeling emotions in my solar plexus, immediately, as they arise, and avoiding my strong tendency to attach a label or a meaning or some type of self-centered story to them. So, I'm practicing staying present to the sensations that arise in my body and taking a moment just to feel them without judging them. It's not easy because my ego is so eager to get its hands on them and create a story or add to an already existing one.

Yes, you're on to him now, that Wile E. Coyote ego of yours!

So here you are, feeling sort of down. Granted, not as good as rarin' to go, but there you are. You're feeling how you're feeling, knowing that you'll be feeling that way for exactly as long as it takes to move on to another, hopefully better-feeling feeling. Here we're showing you via the breadcrumb trail how to shift from those less-good-feeling feelings to a better state of mind. And the first step on that trail is to be okay with how you're feeling in the moment. The next step, assuming you wish to feel better, is to do something different, such as identify and change the negative stories you're telling yourself.

Easier said than done!

No one said anything about easy. But you have been realizing lately that you do have the ability to shift from material world consciousness, where negative feelings run rampant, into that expanded state we're calling the quantum. This realization itself is cause for celebration because you now understand that's where your free will resides and that you're free to go there at will. That is what kept Viktor Frankl alive in the concentration camp. He realized his ability, and the ability inherent in all humans, to transcend the suffering of the material world and jump to the quantum. His body was imprisoned but his spirit was free.

What is called for first is constant vigilance—constant awareness of the negative talk you heap upon yourself. This is the voice of the ego. Even though it is really only doing its job and trying to keep you safe, the results are not good. You are kept safe, but from what? Anything new or exciting or creative. We would ask, is that type of safe life worth living?

Hmm, probably not. But even though I now recognize my ego voice for what it is, I've still had to work hard to loosen its grip on my daily life. I remember maybe twenty years ago when I first became aware of how nasty I was to myself, I was looking at my face in the mirror, observing what appeared to me to be unforgivable facial flaws. I had begun to suspect the damage my ego voice was doing to my psyche, but it took years before I realized I could change that. I wasted many precious years in that vicious cycle.

Not so, Dear One. Every moment was meaningful and sacred because it brought you to the place of awareness where you are now. Even today, there is still remedial mirror work to be done because we still see you at times evaluating your appearance negatively. But you are to be congratulated on the progress you have made thus far. You have so much more affection, appreciation, and regard for yourself than you used to. The work is ongoing, but that is the purpose of time, and it is also your life's purpose: To wake up, recognize, and rejoice in the preciousness of the soul that is you!

A lot of the time, I feel like I'm not using my time on Earth wisely.

Balderdash! You, Dear One, are a flower that is blooming in its own natural, perfect, and inevitable way. There is no need to force a bloom. No added speed is called for. Your rate of unfoldment is just right for you, the Goldilocks speed. What if you were to really get that events in your life are occurring in perfect timing? And that you don't need to change anything or do anything differently? And we mean REALLY get that?

Then I could stop being anxious, stop feeling incorrect, or that somehow, I'm not doing it right. I'd be free to be more wave-y and less particle-y.

Yes! And at that point you could say with your very best French accent, "Laissez les bons temps rouler," couldn't you? And we are here to tell you that you are free to do that at any and every moment of your precious life. That's where quantum jumping comes into play. Humans have written volumes on this topic, although they don't always call it the same thing. This is as it should be because it's the single most important subject to human beings. Every other thing stems from the human's ability to quantum jump from the prison of the material world to the absolute freedom of the quantum world.

There are many teaching aids designed to assist in learning to jump, but meditation is one of the most reliable. It does not often produce overnight results or sudden flashes of enlightenment, but regular practice is the key. In her forty years of meditation practice, Dear One has never experienced any lightning bolts of self-realization. But she does regularly experience relaxation, occasional a-ha moments, and even some brief periods of bliss, but certainly no sudden awakenings of her consciousness.

Do you think it's important to know what your unique purpose is in order to be able to jump?

We would say that jumping is a natural and inevitable occurrence consistent with living a purpose-filled life. Many things have been said on this subject—some helpful, some less so.

Your life's purpose is to be you, as only you can. In that endeavor you cannot fail; are we agreed? We would add that the more authentically you express who you are, the happier you are going to be and the freer you're going to feel. Think of the lucky individuals who are born with such obvious talents in such specific areas that they cannot help but follow that passion throughout their lives. Pursuing God-given talents does not automatically bring an easy, happy life, but it does provide a stable foundation on which to practice being your own precious self. We would say that the more you can strip away those ego-created layers of conditioning and limiting beliefs (insert picture of onion cross section), the better you will be able to express what is uniquely yours to bring to the world.

And speaking of service, please allow us to expand on that a bit. Once individuals are conscious of their role in the Universe, part of the All That Is, and enthused with the spirit of God, they will naturally desire to be of service to the whole. They will understand that giving is receiving and that, in Truth, there is no separate self who does the giving or the receiving. It is all of a piece, a beautiful piece of tapestry where threads of various colors and textures are

interwoven, a piece of clothing that you put on and enjoy
wearing endlessly. Is that not what you were attempting to
do with AngelWear, Dear One? You knew the Truth of your
mission instinctively even then, twenty years ago, although
you could not have expressed it in words.

Well, I actually did try to express it in words. This is what I had
printed on my hang tags:

Let AngelWear remind us that we are spiritual beings
Whose true essence is pure love and light.
May it remind us that I who make the garment and you who wear it
Are not separate, but in Truth, One.
May these remembrances bring healing to us all.

You wrote that in 1997, before you really knew who you
were or really understood the Truth behind the words. You
were in a formative stage, like the caterpillar in the
chrysalis, waiting to transform into a butterfly. You wrote
those words during a personal crisis. Desperately wanting
to believe them, you were reaching out to the nonphysical
for evidence that they were True. We picture you as a
swimmer in troubled water, seas swirling around you. The
Universe threw you a life preserver in the form of a business
through which you could express your undeniable genius
and relentless creativity.

I do see now how AngelWear was a life preserver. I wanted
something to believe in, something that would allow me to believe
in myself. So I threw my heart and soul into it, as if my very life
depended on it. There was never a waking moment when I wasn't
thinking about it or actually working on it, sketching, pattern
making, cutting, sewing samples. You name it. I did it all. I was a
maniac with a mission. I had some good success, but after seven

years, I closed up shop. My clothes weren't selling as they once did, and I didn't want to change my design aesthetic to make them more sellable. I felt lost and alone, abandoned by the Universe. I lost my faith and my sense of purpose. I felt I had failed.

Yes, that was your interpretation. Another option would have been to sit back and gratefully say, "Whew, glad that's over. Nice ride, though!" But you chose to interpret the situation as failure on your part, and your insistence on that has been the cause of much needless suffering in your life. We're not sure that you have yet released that self-criticism you heaped upon yourself when you stopped doing AngelWear. Are you ready to stop now?

I think I finally am ready, after twenty years, to reframe that experience. I'll stop telling the "failure" story and start telling the "what a miracle" story. The Universe threw me a lifeline. I grabbed it, and it kept me afloat for many years. Plus, it gave me confidence because it showed me I could do anything I put my heart and soul into. When I think of it that way, it doesn't sound like failure anymore.

Good decision, Dear One!

Speaking of reframing stories, several of my friends have decided not to get the COVID vaccine, and although that's not a good choice for me, I respect their right to choose it for themselves. I made arrangements to go to the house of a friend who, I was pretty sure, was unvaccinated.

Please, may we jump in here? We know you want to tell the story, but may we recount it from a more quantum perspective?

Take it away.

Picture this: Dear One, cruising along with the top down on her fictional powder blue T-Bird convertible, enjoying the fine weather and fresh air. Suddenly... SCREECH! She is stopped short by a text from her boyfriend telling her that if the friend she's on her way to meet is not vaccinated, she should wear a mask. A logical request, one might say, but not to Dear One. She finds the request directive and controlling. It pushes a button on her movie projector which starts the film containing clips of all the times she has been dominated and dismissed by men. She replays the doormat scenes from her marriage, and scenes from other relationships where she's been diminished and felt unable to defend herself.

And here's that other one where she's sitting on the floor of her bedroom where she's been sent after speaking disrespectfully to Mommy. Four-year-old Joy has so much rage toward Mommy it can't be contained in her small body. She just doesn't know where to put it, but she has learned that it must not, nay, cannot on penalty of death, be expressed out loud. This is an important one because this was the beginning of the strangulation of Joy.

Oh! Here's another scene where she's been bound and gagged. She's about to be burned at the stake as a witch. It's from a previous life, but it's certainly relevant to the present one.

As an aside, but an instructive one we judge, we are suspecting the witch-burning scene arose because Dear One watched several episodes of a television series last night about a female British spy during World War II. It contained many graphic and ugly scenes of violence. Dear One is paying the price for that "entertainment" today. She did, however, learn why it would be good not to do that again. She will endeavor to never again feed herself popcorn laced with cyanide.

Back to the story. Dear One is sitting in the powder blue T-Bird convertible, engine spewing smoke, unable to continue her journey to see her friend because of the mind movies she has projected onto the screen of her consciousness. It's completely taken over her energy and attention and she's stuck in this stinky, smokey stalemate.

"Well," we say in our sprightly, slightly chirpy, and, we are sure, very annoying voice, "What better time than now for a nice plunge into the quantum?" So, we suggest that she jump out of the T-Bird and run to that little lake, the one we just passed in that grove of trees over there, the one that exists in the quantum. The water is clear and clean, has a sizable beach for sunbathing and a smooth sandy bottom without rocks. Towels and cold drinks are provided free at the concession stand. She has conveniently worn a swimsuit under her clothes, so she must merely take off her outerwear and plunge into the refreshingly cool water. Not too hot, not too cold, but just right. Ah, and how refreshing it is! It is all she needs to relax her brains and quit trying to figure things out logically. She needs merely to float on her back and surrender to the protective embrace of the supportive water. Yes, the water holds her up without question. It is not thinking about how to calculate the density of her body or trying to remember the formula for buoyancy. The water's support is really not personal. It would do the same for anyone. It's just a law of nature in action. And the laws of nature are always in action, you see, although outcomes can vary based on circumstances at the local level, which means, really, that anything can happen. Don't you just love the quantum? It's so inclusive.

It is in this state of utter and complete relaxation that she will be able to rewire her brain and reimagine all sorts of possible solutions to her seeming stalemate, which, in

Truth, is not a stalemate at all, because it is very fluid and dynamic, and she can create the outcome she wishes. She now knows that there are an infinite array of possible outcomes and that she need merely ask herself which one she desires. So she asks, and what comes out on top is... drumroll please... that she consider her own feelings first. Her wish is to feel happy in her ability to choose the most loving action and know that she can express herself clearly and kindly to herself and all those involved.

She reflects that her teacher, Noa, is no longer her North Star. Dear One has graduated to the ranks of those most blessed souls who recognize and rely on their own inner guidance and on no one or nothing external. Furthermore, she no longer values the approval of others over her own well-being, yes, even including the approval of her boyfriend. She knows that she can say what she needs to from a place of love, and all will be well. This reassurance gives her the ability to float languidly on her back, eyes shut. Relaxed, refreshed, reenergized.

We are glad this mask-versus-no-mask issue came forward. Yes, indeed, it has allowed us to go to the lake and have a relaxing swim, and by the time we get back to the car, the engine is cool and ready to continue the trip. The Universe is constantly presenting us with opportunities like this one for soul development. Usually, these presents come to us via loved ones, such as close friends, lovers, and family members. And that is why our relationships are so infinitely valuable from a developmental, instructive point of view. Our job is to recognize them as gifts, which—believe you us—is not always easy. And remember to take them to the quantum level where all solutions are possible.

Pliny, please tell the outcome of this scenario.

Dear One arrived at the home of her friend and was greeted warmly. Dear One inquired in a nonjudgmental way about the vaccination status of said friend. Said friend replied no, she was not vaccinated, a fact which Dear One had already intuited. They both put on their masks and had a lively and meaningful conversation. After a time, they said goodbye and Dear One drove back home. End of story. No drama, no trauma, only love. We would judge, however, that there is something extremely exciting in this story, life altering, mind blowing actually, in that it was an opportunity for Dear One to turn off the movie projector and choose another option, the quantum option, of course, with a nice dip in the lake in the bargain.

Each individual has the choice to live in the Truth or deny it and live in the material world instead. Depression and varying degrees and types of mental illness are the result of living with lies, those ego stories characterized by sub-conscious, repressed emotions and unexplored trauma. We would say that any effort to ferret out those furry little creatures is well worth the pain that might be caused by the digging. Yes, let's think of the ego stories as ferrets that love to hide and nest in small places and do mischief in the psyche. One must search diligently to find them, but once found and taken to safety, they become quite harmless. The wise course of action would be to take them to the quantum realm where they may be de-materialized properly, their molecules dissolved. They will be returned to waves of probability, with no harm done to ferrets in the process.

In the past year or so, I've had swallowing problems which my thinking brain has attributed to enlarged tonsils caused by the leukemia, a theory that has been corroborated by others in my online CLL support group. Pliny, what wisdom do you have for me regarding my swallowing problems?

We feel you constricting your throat muscles in reaction to the fear you are experiencing. Have you ever thought about all the untruths you've swallowed in your long life? And we are referring to the nonsense uttered by teachers, government officials, and authorities of all stripes. And what about the nonsense you've swallowed by people who purported to love you, such as parents, lovers, close friends, and ex-husbands? And what about the non-truth from mere acquaintances? Yes, it's been a boatload that Joy has swallowed and now she's surprised that she's having trouble swallowing.

I'd like to stop that. Can you tell me how?

Jumping into the quantum is the only viable solution for this and every other perceived problem that you have now or will ever have. There is nothing to be gained from rummaging around in that musty old rucksack of stored experiences, the one with the old lies and unpleasant images from the past.

Like the one where I was a Black man hung by a group of White men for a crime I didn't commit?

Yes, exactly like that one and the one we mentioned previously where you were bound, gagged, and burned at the stake as a witch. Even though these examples are from previous lifetimes, the feelings are still being carried forward because you have been unable to discharge them. You have not yet found the release valve. (Please insert here an image of an Instant Pot with arrow pointing to the steam release.)

How can I bring up that rage again so I can release it? All I can feel now is fear, but I'm aware that anger is lurking somewhere beneath that.

Yes, in a subterranean pocket of volatile magma, there are noxious gases which you are reluctant to excavate for fear of poisoning yourself and everyone around you. This is your most ambitious project yet, Dear One. Your upbringing has so successfully indoctrinated you in the "be nice" school of thought that it has completely blocked anger in any form. You have not felt healthy anger since age four.

I'm remembering the words of a very wise and spiritually advanced doctor I knew at a hospital I once worked in who told me that her leukemia patients were the nicest people in the world. She had observed that they were often nice to others at their own expense. She didn't say anything about repressed anger, but now I'm connecting the dots and seeing how much sense that makes.

Unfortunately, our culture doesn't give people much help in learning how to express anger in ways that aren't destructive to oneself and others, so what do you recommend, Pliny?

We would prescribe some hypnosis sessions, for starters. That should loosen up some of those neural pathways so that you can begin to entertain those forbidden feelings consciously. Hypnosis bypasses the conscious mind which is a very strict gatekeeper and frequently acts in a manner contrary to our well-being. A good hypnotherapist can assist you to surface those rageful feelings where they may be dealt with and dissipated. And please, don't be thinking that this is not a very spiritual solution to the problem. All solutions are potentially spiritual, and especially those that work.

Getting back to the topic of life purpose, sometimes I feel like I have so many interests and so many things I want to do and have to do that I can't seem to grab hold of what's really essential, such as fulfilling my purpose, so I might as well fill in the time dealing with the trivia that comes in the form of emails and texts so my proverbial decks are clear when I finally get around to doing the important stuff. Does that make sense?

No, it doesn't make sense, but we understand what you mean. Many humans contend with this phenomenon that they term overwhelm. Much of the time, digital devices are contributing to the problem, but are not the sole cause of it. We would like to point out here the obvious solution is to do those things that make you feel good when you're doing them. They are like large arrow-shaped signposts saying, "Life purpose this way." We also know that there are many routine and repetitive tasks that humans must do to maintain their bodies and their surroundings. Although these activities do not seem to be contributing directly to their overall life purpose, they are mandatory and must be done. Our approach to these tasks would be to appreciate the sacredness of each moment of your life, including the time spent brushing teeth and washing dishes. Practice being grateful that you have teeth to brush and dishes to wash. Yes, feel gratitude even for that lovely crusty lasagna pan in your sink—especially that one.

I've been listening to podcasts after I turn off my light at night with the idea of learning more about how to determine and fulfill my life's purpose.

It strikes us that a more direct route might be to merely check with your quantum self but continue. It sounds like you've come to some conclusion.

Last night I listened to Steven Cope on Rick Archer's *Buddha at the Gas Pump*, and they were discussing this topic. My best, but maybe not final, definition of my life's purpose is to create the fullest possible expression of my God self, that is, the best version of myself as a fractal of God's energy and to bring that expression into the physical realm and share it with my family, friends, community, and the world. In other words, to actually embody my purpose, not just contemplate it endlessly. Am I getting warmer, Pliny?

We would say you are red hot! But we would also like to point out that making a distinction between the physical (embodiment) and the mental (contemplation) may not be helpful and could lead to erroneous conclusions. One doesn't have to make a choice between sitting in meditation and taking action. Remember, the quantum is a both/and environment, not an either/or one. We could say that by sitting in meditation, as you have done all these years, you have been preparing yourself to take not just any action; you have been informing yourself to take enlightened action. Aside from this one minor quibble, we put our official stamp of approval on your best-for-now—although maybe-not-final—version of your life's purpose.

Okay, that sounds good to me! What other wisdom do you have to impart regarding quantum jumping? I don't want to get off track too much here, but I'm remembering that the term has been used by others to describe the fact that because there are an infinite number of alternative Universes in the quantum world, one may merely imagine and then jump into one's Universe of choice.

In another version of this hypothesis, Russian scientist Vladimir Raikov experimented in the 1960s with a phenomenon that later came to be known as the Raikov Effect. He showed that under the right conditions and with practice, music students were able to jump from their current level of proficiency to the ability of their favorite virtuoso. The results were astoundingly significant, verifiable, and repeatable, the sine qua non of scientific experimentation. But at the time, the scientific community had no way to explain the results, so they were largely ignored.

We are appreciating Dear One's digression because it has meaning in her own life, its interest is not merely academic. And we will say that this phenomenon is entirely in keeping with another little-known characteristic of a quantum Universe, which holds that in the quantum world, since individuals are not separate from each other, they may easily access characteristics of any other individual of their choosing. Dear One was much taken by the Raikov idea and experimented with it using Itzhak Perlman, her favorite violinist, as the virtuoso. Although we are sorry to report that her technical skill level is still not equal to that of Itzhak, she has learned to play with much more heart, something that Itzhak is known for. She is allowing herself to feel her emotions more while playing and easing up on her critical voice. Her playing has improved considerably as a result of her experimentation. She has also found more enjoyment in listening to music, both recorded and live, because now her focus has shifted from listening for mistakes to listening with her heart, open and ready to receive emotional impressions.

Just to be clear, music and other forms of artistic expression can be effective aids in quantum jumping.

What role does creativity play in fulfilling one's life purpose?

Hold on just a minute—we feel you trying to anticipate our words. Will you please stop it. We like it when you have absolutely no idea what we are going to say. This makes you nervous, but please, just relax and trust us. We will not disappoint. Creativity is nothing more or less than imagining and materializing from the quantum, where all possibilities can be drawn upon. Dear One knows well the feeling of being in that state and just letting ideas pour forth. Nothing is, was, or ever shall be more exciting than this creative process.

Remember designing your AngelWear clothing collections from a quantum perspective? Remember the pink pansy jacquard patterned cotton happi coat with the cream silk side tie? It was pure genius, pure you! Those ideas were right there, ready to roll, onto your sketch pad then onto the pattern paper and were finally materialized in fabric form. It was only when you became fearful, pressed for time, or worried about the scarcity of resources that you were unable to access the plenitude of ideas in the All That Is.

During those good times you felt you were channeling ideas from someplace outside yourself. Artists often say that the inspiration seems to come from a source other than their own personal consciousness. Well, that's the beauty of it, don't you see? As part of a quantum consciousness, you have every right to access creative ideas that don't belong solely to you but are part of the collective consciousness. From that perspective they're as much yours as anyone's. Everything belongs to everybody, and nothing belongs to no one. That's what's behind the Raikov experiments too. We may have some other interesting commentary on creativity, so stay tuned.

Chapter 9
More Advice on Quantum Jumping

I've had a home interior design job I've been working on these past few days, feverishly actually, and I've missed a few days of conversation with you, Pliny. Sorry.

We've missed speaking with you but find it so endearing that when you are working intently on a project such as the design project you have now, you are, for all practical purposes, insensate to any input we might have for you. We would like to suggest that you widen your focus, your aperture, your range of field, to one broad enough to encompass our input, especially when you are working on a creative project. We just might be of assistance to you.

Yes, I understand... oops, I interrupted you.

Yes, you did. We were about to suggest that you dial back the intensity gauge just a notch or two, you know, the gauge that's part of the creative energy-powered apparatus of yours. The apparatus is a sort of Rube Goldberg-inspired piece of equipment that's uniquely yours. It wouldn't work for anyone but you. Everyone has their own version of this apparatus, by the way. It's their own personal creative engine that's been gifted to them by the Universe.

One more thing before you interrupt again: You, Dear One, have been gifted with an exceptionally powerful creative engine, and we find that there is much unused potential in it. We suggest you find a creative outlet for all this potential. This book is one worthy outlet, but we see others coming your way as well.

What else am I supposed do to?

Aha! There you go again, trying to mine us for answers that only your own excavations can extract. And don't think there is something you are required to do. Think of it as searching for treasure more precious than gold. It would take all the fun out of it if we were to tell you where to start digging. But we will give some suggestions.

Think of your fondest hope, your heart's desire, the place your creative genius loves to go when you daydream. Your AngelWear clothing line was not far from the spot you should start digging. Simply let yourself be filled with love for that concept and click your heels twice. And there you are, not back in Kansas, but in that wonderful place of sharing your artistic genius with the world.

[Later]

I want to clarify something regarding the role of meditation in quantum jumping. Just about everything I read says that meditation is an essential part of spiritual practice because it enables the mind to quiet and clears the access to one's God self, intuitive wisdom, whatever you want to call it. Yet there are so many people who say they just can't do it. What's up with that?

We would like to affirm that meditation can, indeed, provide those benefits to the individual. We shudder to think of the state of Dear One's psyche had she not been meditating since 1982. Ah hahaha. We're just trifling with you, Dear One. But might there be a smidge of truth there?

The problem arises when meditation becomes a prescript-tion, a set of instructions to be followed, rather than a description. We prefer the descriptive approach, and by that we mean a detailing of all the pleasurable effects of the practice: that feeling of ease, relaxation, the calming of the incessant mind chatter and, yes, even bliss that can and frequently does come with the practice of meditation. However, humans often feel that they're not doing it right, which is a natural conclusion for those living in a dualistic paradigm. You're either doing it right or you're not, so says the egoic mind.

But this dualistic point of view is not helpful. Dear One suffers from it greatly in many different contexts. It was strongly reinforced by her training as a librarian. She wants to do things correctly, by the book, so to speak. So she reads the book and does what other people have determined to be the absolute best way, completely oblivious to those delicious intuitive hits she often receives but doggedly ignores.

We are here to tell her that there is no book, and if there were a book, we would toss it out the window immediately (depending, of course, on who or what is under the window, we wouldn't want to injure any unfortunate passersby, would we?) But who cares if you're following the rules because in Truth, there are no actual rules. That's a rhetor-ical question, so no need to put a question mark at the end.

What's important is the experience of the practice, which can and frequently does cause benefits in the practitioner's mind and body. So, our advice to those on the fence of meditative indecision would be "Shut up and meditate."

We don't mean to be harsh, but please don't tell us you're not doing it because your mind is too active, your body too restless, or you don't have the time. If you want to develop a meditation practice, or any spiritual practice for that matter, and you see enough benefit there, you can do it. Don't think about the rules, think about the benefits. Picture yourself as one of those aforementioned remarkable cows in the Alpine meadow. You're munching away on that sweet, fragrant grass. The bell around your neck is tinkling slightly as you chew. The sun is shining down, and a slight breeze is ruffling the fur on your back (you're a furry cow). If you can feel that, you're on your way to a meditation practice. And don't let any meditation expert tell you otherwise.

I had a thought during my morning meditation that I think relates to the ability to quantum jump.

We are all ears.

I was noticing how my busy mind likes to take feelings and sensations and attach words, values, and interpretations to them. For instance, this morning I had a twitching feeling in my finger and watched as my mind diagnosed it as a symptom of progressive neurological illness. Is that weird?

No, that's normal. It's just your egoic mind doing what it loves to do and what it gets paid to do, which is to take sensory input, scan its vast storehouse of impressions called the subconscious and come up with a match. If it can't find an exact match, it will present something close and declare, "Ah! This same thing (or something close) happened before and here's how we reacted. Let's react the same way we did before and hopefully we'll get out of here alive."

So how do I stop my monkey mind from doing that? And by monkey mind I'm referring to the relentless and incessant flood of thoughts and impressions that seems to be beyond my power to control.

Any good meditation teacher will tell you not to attempt to stop the thoughts. Don't chastise yourself about having them, but once you become aware of them, merely return to whatever meditation technique you are practicing, such as being aware of breath or repeating a mantra. As some wise person said, "You can't stop the birds from flying through your hair, but you can stop them from making a nest there." We are enjoying the image of a bird's nest atop Dear One's head.

I've noticed that you like to use natural elements as metaphors in these conversations, such as birds and those remarkable cows. Why is it that nature feels so soothing, healing, you might say?

Elementary, my dear Dear One! Nature reminds us that we are all of a piece, part of the All That Is, part of the collective consciousness. Is it not comforting to remember that in our most essential state we are part of something so grand, so divinely conceived, so exquisitely crafted and so intelligently executed it defies comprehension?

Don't you just love it when you catch a glimpse of a natural vista so panoramic and vast that your heart leaps up into your throat? How about the Grand Canyon, El Capitan, the broad Missouri, just to mention a few examples in the United States alone. And how many such mindblowers are there throughout this world, not to mention the entire Universe? And this awe reaction is not restricted to only vast panoramas. Think about the delicate wings of a hummingbird or the intricate formations of small flowers. Yes, how can one not be lifted up by the mere existence of such exquisite forms in nature? That is why practices such as forest bathing and just spending time outdoors anywhere are so healing. They remind you of who you are and bring you peace, affirming your essential nature, which is both a part of the All That Is and, at the same time, a unique representative of the totality. Pretty awesome, we would say!

Agreed.

And why, pray tell, would you think that your body is any less awesome, intelligent, complex, and completely worthy of the same sacred devotion as the flowers? We notice that sometimes humans lose sight of this fact when they are not feeling well. Indeed, the Western medical model encourages this forgetting. The focus is on what's gone wrong in the body, and the subsequent application of some outside agent to correct the problem, such as pharmaceuticals, radiation, surgery, etc. We are here to tell you that symptoms of illness arise when the host is ready and able to hear and clear the problem, which is always an energy blockage of some type. Illness arises as part of the body's efforts to bring to light unwanted negative beliefs that are hindering the soul's progression. It is the soul's desire to wake up and express its purpose with creativity and joy in a body that's vitally alive.

[The next day]

Pliny, for a long time, maybe since before my divorce, I've had difficulty envisioning my future. I've been thinking that this may be a problem because if I don't know where I want to go, it will be difficult to get there, no? Should I be cultivating a more definite picture of what my future looks like?

We understand that since her diagnosis twelve years ago, Dear One has been reluctant to picture her future because she thinks that if she dies of the disease, she might be disappointed in herself. We are not making this up! She really thinks that. This is a fine example of the contortions and convolutions that an ingenious ego mind can get up to in order to justify its existence. (Please insert a drawing of a pretzel here.)

Dear One's ego has been telling her that she must guard against the feeling that her life has been a disappointment both to herself and to her fellow humans. We came to assure her that she can let her guard down and dismiss this thought as sheer lunacy. Nothing could be further from the truth. She has led a creative and intellectually daring life. She has dared to do many things in service to her soul's growth and for the advancement of humanity. In truth, every human life is a success from a cosmic standpoint, even though it may not appear so on the material level. If any of our Dear Readers are feeling the same way as Dear One, please be advised that it is unwarranted and stop it immediately.

So then, Dear One, if the burden of disappointing yourself is lifted, what will you choose as a future? Go ahead, launch one of those rockets of desire, as Abraham Hicks puts it.

Hmmm, here's a scenario I love: My lymph nodes gradually shrink, my lymphocyte count goes back to normal, and soon no trace of leukemia can be found in my body. My doctors are speechless. That is, they don't say anything because they don't know how to explain it. People just don't recover from this type of leukemia, according to Western medicine. However, I know what to say, and I shout it from the rooftops: "Consciousness creates matter, folks! We can heal our illnesses with our consciousness." And I carry on writing books, doing podcast interviews, and television appearances. I'm never nervous about these events because, frankly, I don't give a rip about what people think of me. I've learned to trust my guides, including you, Pliny, and I continue to converse with you every day because it gives me such peace and clarity.

Wow, I'm excited about that future!

Well, you should be, Dear One, because it is what your heart desires, and it is for this that your soul has come into a body this lifetime. You are cocreating your future with the All That Is at every moment, so why not go for what you want? Don't hold back and, above all, don't forget to write! We do have one small suggestion to make regarding the picturing of your future. Do not predicate the fame and fortune part of your scenario on eradicating your illness. Doing that puts the spotlight on what you don't want—that is, the disease.

Here's how we would rewrite the story: You publish this book and go on to enjoy great success in whatever way you choose to define that. And in so doing, you are spending not a smidgen of time thinking about whether or not your illness is cured. You're just enjoying the ride, loving yourself and others, and one day you wake up knowing that your illness is gone. Healing can be seen as a side effect of creating and loving your joyful life, in which your focus is so totally on the living that there is no energy for concern about illness and symptoms.

I want to thank you so much for this wonderful session! I am truly blessed to know you.

We share that feeling with you.

[The next day]

Are there other tips and techniques you can give to help me to practice quantum jumping?

Well, we are glad you used the word practice because it acknowledges that, like all skills in the material world, it takes time to learn. Didn't someone say that it took ten-thousand hours or ten years of practice to master a skill?

Yes, someone said that, and we have no idea if it is true, but it suits our purposes here so we will use it.

The point is that when one is working with something as dense as matter, it takes a certain amount of time to affect it if those efforts are made on the material level. It is much more effective, that is, less onerous and time-consuming, if done energetically, and by that we mean in the conscious- ness of the jumper. So we're suggesting that you not go out to the athletic field and practice long jumping or anything of that nature; rather, make the jump in your consciousness. And to do that well, it is best to prepare oneself with some warm-ups, such as breathing exercises and heart opening calisthenics. Dear One has some experience in that area, so why don't you hold forth a little for the benefit of our Dear Readers?

Wow, I get to hold forth? Alrighty then.

Back in the summer of 2016, I tried an experiment with cannabis oil and something called the Rick Simpson Protocol as a cure for my leukemia. The protocol required, over the course of several weeks, working up to ingesting one gram of cannabis oil every twenty-four hours for three months. You can Google it to get the details of the protocol if you're interested. You'll find reports of people using this regimen to cure various types of cancer. I can't vouch for their authenticity, but I was interested enough to give it a try. With the help of a friend who lives in Oregon and knows reputable growers, I followed the protocol meticulously, and let me tell you, it was not easy! In any case, it didn't cure my leukemia that summer, but it did give me a gift beyond measure. It helped me learn how to open my heart at will. I had learned through years of conditioning that it just wasn't safe to walk around with an open heart, and so I shut my emotions down pretty severely and effectively. I didn't feel much of anything, neither happy nor sad emotions, and my life had become pretty cardboard; and there is no juice in cardboard.

During the protocol, I began noticing that I could actually feel emotions, and I began experimenting with this new-found ability. I discovered I could go from zero to ten on the emotional scale, from flat to full-out sobbing, in about thirty seconds. I was, and still am, so proud of myself! For someone who was not used to feeling things, this was a huge triumph. I could also use my consciousness to open my heart by thinking of something or someone I loved. I pictured my heart as a lotus blooming in my chest, and I still use this image. After a while I could generalize this open-hearted feeling to other people and situations. For me, thoughts and images of dogs were also effective stimuli since I love dogs so much.

Prior to my cannabis experience, I had experimented with a HeartMath Institute technique similar to the one I'm describing, but the addition of cannabis seemed to be just what I needed to dissolve the blockages around my heart. Since completing the protocol, I no longer need to take cannabis to engage my emotions, but I still take time every day to practice opening my heart. I can still cry at the drop of a hat, and do so frequently, sometimes to the discomfort of those around me. I don't care though, because it feels so good.

I do have a confession to make, however. Yesterday I went to my local chain grocery store with a shut-down heart, and I didn't notice it until I got back in the car and was thinking how much I dislike going there. I try to avoid going to this particular store, but it's very conveniently located near my home, so I wind up shopping there weekly. It carries sad organic produce, and the people who are working there always seem unhappy. Because I'm an empath, I can feel how much they don't want to be there. Then it occurred to me that maybe the source of the problem was somewhere in my vicinity, as Pliny has pointed out to me previously, and when I checked in with my heart, I saw that it was closed. I had been just trying to get in and out of the place as quickly as I could and forgot about my heart. Big mistake.

There is only one ray of sunshine at this store, and he is a young man who collects the carts in the parking lot and makes an effort to engage customers in upbeat conversations. A few weeks ago, he told me my T-shirt was his favorite color, and I instantly felt better. Here is a man who is collecting grocery carts but knows something big. His attitude makes his job bearable—no, probably more than that, it probably makes it satisfying and maybe even fulfilling. It's even contagious. Everyone around him just feels better.

I've decided to carry out an experiment, sort of like the ones advocated by Pam Grout in her books on the quantum realm. Before entering the store, I'm going to prepare myself by doing a heart opening meditation. I'm going to be conscious of beaming love and light to all the poor fruits and vegetables, employees, and other shoppers. I will be maintaining that energy even in the midst of the prevailing unhappiness, just like my friend and role model, the shopping cart guy out in the parking lot.

> *Brilliant idea, Dear One. We are glad to see you putting into practice our prescriptions. And thank you, for your reportage on the cannabis experiment. It will be instructive for many. Humans in the future will not know any other way of living. They will live in a constant state of open hearted-ness. They will be walking around that way, eyes open, hearts open. It will not be restricted to practice sessions. Everyone will be ever so much safer and happier that way. As a caveat, we would say that we do not recommend that everyone take cannabis as a means to this end. Dear One's unique physiology benefited from the added jolt that cannabis gave her nervous system. It is not so for everyone.*

Last night a bunch of us got together at Noa's house because she reminded us that we needed to stay connected to ourselves and to each other. It was my turn on the table and everyone's healing energy was directed toward me. It felt so good, I think because I felt so loved and supported. Why are relationships so healing for humans?

At the risk of repeating ourselves, we would remind you again that in the quantum, All is One. Once you get that as a felt experience and not just a platitude, you want to be in that Oneness state all the time. The seeming disparate fractals that are Noa and the other individuated souls that are her students are, in Truth, part of the collective consciousness, and that's where healing takes place. Healing does not take place in isolation, where those disparate entities seem to be separate from one another. Relationships show you facets of yourself that you may not have been aware of. Fractals have a way of reminding each other who they really are, and in a very immediate and sometimes annoying way. That's the beauty of relation-ships. May we inquire how you are feeling today, the day after the meeting?

I can't remember a time when I've felt more cared for and cherished. And the truly miraculous thing about it was that I felt worthy of that outpouring of love and not the least bit ashamed to admit that I have an illness, something that has plagued me in the past.

Yes, we second all those lovely emotions. You are becoming more aware of the need to involve others in your healing. You are experiencing a new appreciation of the ACIM quote "When I am healed, I am not healed alone." How you've interpreted that in the past is that you do the healing work by yourself and then offer it to others, but in Truth, that's not how it works. One does not heal in isolation. It's a process that requires other humans to accomplish. We are so glad Dear One is feeling loved, but she is losing wattage and needs to nap now.

Wait, I'm not ready for sleep yet! This is really interesting to me because I have always seen myself as pretty much a loner, and I haven't been particularly social or open to accepting help from others. When I'm sick or hurt, I just want to be left alone. My Human Design chart reflects that tendency. My profile is that of the heretical hermit, and my 32/5 life path in numerology shows that I'm working on issues of independence and interdependence in this lifetime. It seems that I haven't gotten it totally worked out, because under stress, I lean toward isolation rather than connection with others.

Yes, and this is why you're still alive, Dear One. You haven't gotten it worked out and you most likely never will. We say this not to discourage you, but to diminish that unrealistic desire for perfection.

While we're on this topic, I'm interested to know your opinion of the discipline called Human Design.

There is much truth and value in the system of soul analysis known as Human Design, but what is important is that it affirms you and your life experience and produces feelings of understanding, acceptance, and even empowerment. Additionally, if approached artistically, Human Design brings into relief the crystalline, intricate nature of the human soul, much like a kaleidoscope arranges and re-arranges patterns of shapes and colors for the entertainment and pleasure of the viewer. We are looking into yours right now and seeing how the beautifully colored pieces move and then coalesce to form a unique symmetrical design. It is a thing of beauty, just as it is for every living soul. Human Design can help individuals understand the themes that will be expressed during their lifetimes because each lifetime, the soul chooses a different pattern through which it expresses its uniqueness and its divinity.

We know it is tempting for Dear One to go down the rabbit hole of thought by analyzing the technical aspects of her Human Design chart. Although some analysis is necessary to derive value from the system, please don't overdo it. Analyze enough to feel the genius of the Creator. Study as much as it takes to get that feeling of reverence for self and the sacredness of your journey this lifetime. Then, back off and just bask in the wonder and mystery of it all.

After a while your soul decides it's done enough for one lifetime and that it's time to move on.

Time to die, you mean?

We hate using that word because it's so charged for all humans. You know, of course, that your soul never dies, it just transitions from human-based energy to spirit-based energy. Yes, souls do decide to transition at a point where they feel that the work they've done is sufficient, even though they often are aware that there will be other lives where the same themes will need to be brought forward to be worked on again. And there is certainly no shame involved in that, the deferral of karma to the next lifetime, that is.

My Vedic astrology reading yesterday indicated that I have the opportunity this lifetime to reach enlightenment and not have to return to the Earth plane again. What do you think about that?

We don't think much about that, either in a good or bad way. If it pleases you to think of reaching enlightenment this lifetime, we applaud that (insert drawing of clapping hands) and say go for it! However, attaining enlightenment should not be seen as a goal to be striven for and attained. Focus instead upon enjoying this one precious life you have been given. Yes, you are still fully alive after all these years; your body is clearly not dead yet. And yes, we are suggesting you call forth that ebullient unbounded energy that fully expresses the true nature of Joy.

Can you say a few words about the role of breathing as it pertains to quantum jumping?

Yes, we think it is a good idea. Ah hahaha! We just love ourselves, don't you?

Immensely.

We do not mean to make light of the important role of breath in connecting the soul to the quantum field. Certainly, breathing is essential to life and, we might add, practiced so universally and with such great regularity that it is often overlooked as a vehicle to transcend the ego mind. When done as a mindful practice, conscious breathing can lead to a quieting of the monkey mind and the introduction of a calmer, more stabilized physiology.

When you refer to monkey mind, I picture the monkeys that I saw in the forests around Ubud in Indonesia. Their sharp little eyes would study the tourists, searching for shiny objects or other items of interest that might, perhaps, be traded for bananas. By the way, I recently heard a supposedly true story about a monkey who stole a camera from a tourist and took it to the open market to trade for bananas.

Dear One heard that story yesterday from her Vedic astrologer friend, Robert, and just had to repeat it. See how indulgent and accommodating we are? Plus, we do not want Dear One to feel stifled in any way. That is a familiar and particularly onerous energetic pattern for her.

Back to our original topic, which was using the breath in quantum jumping. As Vipassana meditators know, conscious breathing is effective in quieting the mind. You can even use the breath as a momentary pick-me-up when feel-

ing stuck, out of sorts, or fearful. Breathing consciously leads one by the hand to the present moment. Take just one deep breath and revel in the present moment. Oh heck, take a few and really feel better. Or, better yet, sit yourself down and turn off your phone and just notice your breath for a while. You'll be ever so glad you did, and you'll return to your busy business feeling refreshed, knowing that all is well and that you are well and safe in the loving arms of the Universe.

This discussion is so relaxing, it's gotten me ready for my own meditation session this morning. Will I see you on the other side?

We are with you always, Dear One, whether or not we're in a dictation session. You may access our wisdom at any time, any place. You can dispense with the idea that there is some formula that must be followed in order to connect with us. You need not turn around, jump up and down, or even stand on your head in order to invoke us. None of that about which you are currently reading concerning the "correct" way to do channeled writing pertains to us. Yes, perhaps there are entities which prefer to be cajoled and catered to in that manner, but we are not among them. We are just your no-nonsense, bread-and-butter, everyday discarnate collective energies known as Pliny the Elder whose only wish is to serve you and the All That Is in the highest and best way possible. Put the book away, Dear One, write your own!

[The next day]

Pliny, what reassurance do you have for our Dear Readers who are living in pain or otherwise suffering from intractable illness?

We are honored to be in their presence—those souls who have chosen advancement through illness, pain, and suffering. We would like to suggest that in the face of pain and suffering a wider focus be invoked. We also acknowl-

edge the difficulty some have in getting to a wider, focused awareness, the place we have been calling in this text the quantum consciousness, especially if the body is wracked by pain or experiencing other dire physical symptoms. To those souls we would say "Yes, the body is in pain at the moment, but see if you can reach beyond the dysfunction to that expanded place of peace where respite is possible." Trust in the benevolence of the Universe is essential. Sometimes a relaxation into the All That Is may be possible and other times not. Either way, no shame, no blame. Entirely okay. It's enough just knowing that there's a part of you that can transcend the symptoms. We hope there is some comfort in knowing that.

You brought up the subject of trust, and I had a question for you on that topic.

Be our guest.

I read something in Mark Nepo's *Book of Awakening* this morning that rang true to me. To paraphrase, he said that humans relax into trusting the Universe only after they have totally exhausted themselves on the material level with egoic efforts.

Yes, Dear One, that rang true for you because that is the story you have written with your body, as dictated by your overarching, overachieving egoic mind. But now you are awakening, and your body is prompting you to write a different story. By the way, the telling of a new story can result in the creation of an artistic masterpiece. Be it musical, visual, written, or another type of creative endeavor not normally classified as artistic, when inspired by the All That Is, such an awakening can produce results that are felt and acknowledged by humans to be master-pieces. This book will be in that category.

Recently I've been thinking about how trusting in oneself is related to trusting in the Universe.

Here we are engaging in some hair splitting because as you well know, you are not in any way separate from the Universe. You're a fractal, remember? And to imagine that you're not immediately sets up a problematic proposition. Implicit in your trust in the Universe is trust in yourself, and once you grasp that wholeness feeling, all doubt and questioning cease.

To address a few practical considerations, we would say that trust is essential to healing because it eliminates that human tendency toward anxiousness regarding what could and should be done in the face of illness. By trusting, you are validating your own ability to receive intuitive advice from the All That Is, resulting in the highest and best outcomes for you. In addition, we would say that trust is an essential part of the creative process, which is part and parcel of the healing process. You, as creator, know that you can rely on, and relax into, the support of the All That Is. "Et voilà!" as the French say when they don't know what else to say. In this case it means, "Ah, there you have it!"

I was wondering about that, I mean, how do I know which self-care routines are "right" for my body and will contribute to my healing? I'm struck by how many things I think I have to do related to my physical health. You're saying I should just trust my intuition, and all will be well?

Yes, but that's only part of the answer. We want to congratulate you on taking daily walks around the neighborhood. You get to enjoy the fresh air, flowers, trees, and yesterday Dear One met an adorable puppy that she hadn't seen before, one that made her heart swell with love. Such are a few of the benefits of daily walks. We suggest that you evaluate self-care routines by the degree to which they activate your pleasure molecules, which Dear One thinks might be called dopamine or serotonin but is not sure. Another example is her yoga practice. She loves the feelings of peace, balance, and centeredness that yoga seems to engender. Why not focus on the feelings and see those pleasure molecules circulating throughout your body?

Here's another one: Does she not enjoy rocking out to those '60s songs of her youth as she jumps on her jumping device? Yes, she does. And we know it is called a trampoline, we were just being cute.

You're cute anyway, with or without trying. I get what you're saying, though. Focus on the enjoyment, and don't try to figure it out with brains.

Precisely.

Another topic which I think belongs in the quantum jumping chapter is that of mindfulness, and by that, I mean being in the present moment.

Ah yes, our chapter would not be complete without the inclusion of consideration of the present moment. We like to apply the phrase "the generous present moment," although it does come and go rather quickly, like a little firefly. As soon as your mind registers the fact that there's a small bug with a blinking light on its tail darting about in the darkness, it's gone, which is a good reason to not even attempt to register it or experience it with the thinking mind.

Now I'm wondering if fireflies even exist anymore. I think that as kids we called them lightning bugs, and on hot summer nights in Pennsylvania, we captured them and put them in mason jars and covered the top with aluminum foil, making sure to poke holes in the foil so the bugs could survive overnight. It was pretty magical seeing a jar full of tiny blinking lights; however, they would all be dead by morning.

And in the unlikely event that there are children reading this treatise, let us say we are not condoning this practice of killing innocent bugs purely for entertainment. Perhaps it is practices such as this that have led to their near extinction.

But enough digression. Back to the present moment. What makes the present moment so generous is that it is the only place where you can rewrite the script of your movie. Thinking of the past restricts you to the plots of those old movies that your ego mind created based on prior experiences and are mostly untrue and unhelpful. And thinking of unfortunate future events as they are created by the egoic mind, which has a tendency to awfulize, is equally unhelpful. Whenever you're thinking, you're watching either re-runs or horror movies. The only good thing about them is that they're familiar, we grant you that; however, familiarity in the form of stuckness cannot really be called good, can it?

What about the idea that by thinking about the future in a positive way you can manifest the things and circumstances that you want?

Yes, there is truth to that proposition, but for it to be effective all senses must be on board and operational. And, perhaps most importantly, you must feel the emotions connected with that joyous outcome, not just think about them with your thinking brain. That subconscious mindset will produce those bouncing, dancing pleasure molecules that can and do affect change in the material.

But we ask, and please be honest here, how often do your thoughts of the future involve the anticipation of what you do want versus the dread associated with what you don't want? We think we know the answer, and that is why we are extolling the virtues of the present moment in order to stay out of the morass afore referred to as Camp Swampy.

Okay, just as you suspected, I'm more likely to be thinking of the future in terms of fear rather than happy anticipation. But I've always had trouble being in the present, and as much as I resonate with and appreciate the message delivered by Eckhart Tolle in *The Power of Now*, I've felt that I never really understood how to do it.

Yes, you have tried, and tried, and tried, and tried, and tried. Dear One gets an A for effort but has missed the bus. Here, we are going to make another of our profoundly profound pronouncements: First, you must jump on the bus—jump into the quantum. Realization of the present moment can only be accomplished at the quantum level, where every moment is the present moment. It is where experience in the form of felt sensations is happening and the egoic mind is not evaluating or trying to create a movie script. Dear One is at this very moment in her dense particle-like state and is trying to embody the present moment and is feeling unsuccessful. She is just not feeling wavy. Give it up for the moment, Dear One. You are sensing the truth of what we have just imparted and that is enough for now. Another meditation session will set things to rights.

[Later]

Pliny!

Yes, we are here.

I just got it during my meditation! Being in the present moment is the same thing as being in the quantum! Why didn't you just say that in the first place?

A careful rereading of the transcript will show that we did, indeed, say that, but in a way that you were unable to comprehend at the time. Your egoic mind was wanting to make the simple truth into something complex and requiring effort. And you know what your egoic mind likes to make when it takes truth and mixes it with a bunch of gobbledygook? It makes it into something like mud, except it begins with an s and ends with a t. Do you know what we mean?

Yes, I do know exactly what you mean. I'm so happy that now I finally can grasp how to be present in the moment. You've explained it in a context that's familiar to me.

One word of advice: Don't take this new epiphany and try to analyze it with your thinking mind because you know the end product, don't you? Yes, you do. Your thinking mind takes a complex topic and reduces it to something it can understand and hold up for all to see and say in a self-congratulatory manner, "How great am I? I got the right answer!"

May we change the subject now?

Please do.

I was listening to a *Buddha at the Gas Pump* podcast again last night and the interviewee was a woman who had a profound near-death experience. She brought up the subject of gratitude and I was wondering about the role gratitude plays in healing.

Hmm, we are detecting a whiff of tit-for-tat, that is, a bit of a transactional approach to the subject, a tendency prevalent in humans, many of whom were horse traders in previous lives. The proposition goes like this: I will express my undying gratitude to you (God) and also devote my life to being grateful to you (God), if you will just heal me of my illnesses. Does this feel familiar to you, Dear One?

A smidge.

What would be ever so much more joyful, not to mention more effective, is if the remembrance and appreciation of one's blessings were all that was requested, with no ask involved. Where that takes you is straight back to Lake Gratitude where it's late summer and the water is bathtub warm. You are floating on your back, gazing into a cloudless blue sky, feeling buoyant, supported, and optimistic. You are thinking lovingly of your family and friends and feeling appreciation for all of your life, in fact. You realize that you lack for nothing. The Universe has provided everything you need to lead a purposeful life. End of scene. Amen.

Yes, that's lovely, and how is it related to healing?

It isn't, really, except that you notice after having bathed in Lake Gratitude several times that your symptoms seem to be subsiding. Or maybe they completely go away after just one dip. We are not playing the causation card here. We prefer the correlation card. A healthy body is correlated with living a purposeful, engaged life that's filled with appreciation for all that one has.

[The next day, New Year's Eve]

Pliny, it's the last day of what for me has been an incredible year. And keeping in mind my lessons from Lake Gratitude, I'm so grateful to have met you. Our conversations have been both life-affirming and, I think, even lifesaving. I feel like I've made more spiritual progress this year than in my whole entire life, and that's been a long time. Seventy-six years to be exact.

Hey, but who's counting? We often feel you discounting yourself or apologizing because of your advanced age. We would like to point out just a few things to counter that viewpoint. Do you see how you've maintained your adventurous spirit and your open mind throughout the years? You've always been excited by new ideas and new ventures and hardly ever say no to a possibility because you're afraid. Your thinking has not become solidified with age as happens to many of your age mates. Likewise, your body is remarkably flexible and fit in spite of some past neglect and shall we say (ahem), overindulgence. We have not checked the length of your telomeres lately, but we picture them long and wavy, like those of a child. And long may they wave, Dear One, and that will be just as long as is needed to accomplish your divine purpose. After that, you won't need them anymore.

We are pleased to see that now that you understand the importance of maintaining your previously mentioned Chitty Chitty Bang Bang on a regular basis. We are feeling that the neglect and overindulgence is a thing of the past. We are aware you are a Taurus, and that you believe that overindulgence is part of your astrological makeup, or so you have been told, and you have created your physical reality based on that thought. But we also know (and know that YOU know) self-love trumps all manner of excess and, yes, even astrological tendencies.

We also would like to congratulate you on your persever- ance in getting this book written and available to the myriad of souls who will benefit from its content. This has been no small accomplishment, and without your unflagging atten- tion and hard work it would not have happened. Yes, we know the work has not yet been published, but the train is on the tracks and is barreling downhill. It now has not only the forces of inertia and gravity behind it, but it also has the support of the angelic realms whose only mission is to love and support humans. The particles of possibility are form- ing molecules of matter at warp speed, and it is now unstoppable.

Dear One is thinking now of The Polar Express, *a movie she watched this Christmas season. Yes, just like* The Polar

Express *movie, this book will remind readers of the importance of belief in things unseen, such as love, and connection to others, and connection to God. What could be a more hopeful and upbeat message to bring to yourself and your fellow humans this new year? Please blow that two-toned train whistle now. We are coming through!*

Epilogue
Tips on Reading This Book

Shauna, Dear One's book coach, has suggested that it might be helpful to give our Dear Readers some tips on how to read this book and perhaps make this somewhat unorthodox treatise more useful. Dear One has, of course, passed this assignment along to us as she thinks it sounds tedious and has very little appetite for advice giving in any form.

That is precisely our position as well. We don't want to do it. Hardly ever are we in a prescriptive mood; that is, we don't like to tell people what to do or how to do it. We are especially resistant to telling our Dear Readers how, when, or where to read the masterpiece that is this book. We prefer, rather, to let people do their own thing: To read it at their own pace, to read it in the bathtub (yes, you may), to start at the end and read forward, or to pick pages to read at random, like picking cards from the tarot deck with the idea that something especially relevant for them will show up.

Here are a few more ideas about how to use this book: Place the book on the floor, put one foot on top of it and see if you can balance on one leg (tree pose) on top of it. Or, you could go outside, open the book at the approximate middle, put a dab of peanut butter on the page and watch to see if ants or other insects are attracted to it. Now THAT would be very instructive, perhaps more so than actually reading the contents.

Wow, you've really dug in your heels! You're as stubborn as I am, aren't you?

Let us remind you that we ARE you, and thus identical in every way. We are merely echoing your strong resistance to Shauna's suggestion, well-intentioned as it may be.

Well, if you don't have any advice about how to read this book, do you want to offer any observations or maybe give some ideas about how readers might enjoy this book?

Yes, when you put it that way, it's much more palatable. We are even thinking of putting some of that peanut butter on a few crunchy celery sticks and munching on them as we proceed.

We appreciate that some readers will enjoy the book mainly for its comedic or entertainment value. We have, at every turning, attempted to proceed in the direction of lighthearted-edness. Humans suffering from chronic illness don't need any more prescriptions, be they pharmaceutical or behave-ioral or dietary. There are many well-meaning individuals in the world who want to prescribe for you what to do to get well. If we did have an Rx pad and pen (which we don't) we would write on it Lighten Up, 3x/day with meals (or without meals. Hell, take it whenever you want).

Did you guffaw, laugh, chuckle, chortle, or merely smile a little, Dear Reader? If so, we are deliriously happy. Did you get a whiff of the expanse of possible futures available to you? Of your immense creative power? Did you get the feeling that you could call your own shots, set your own direction, captain your own ship? If you have felt the energy behind any of those cliches, we have accomplished our objective. We are complete. Thank you for humoring us and for letting us humor you.

We hope that some readers will appreciate our bold venture into the scientific realm, our melding of current quantum scientific knowledge with our (Pliny's) quantum vision and Dear One's understanding of the metaphysical. They will appreciate our courage in taking on issues which are, by their very nature, impossible for the human thinking mind to comprehend. We have used colorful language and evoked interesting images to escape the thinking mind in order to jump into an expanded consciousness where everything is known and knowable. We would measure the success of this book by the extent to which we have been successful in facilitating that jumping.

We are also hoping that some readers will benefit from reading the books mentioned in our conversations, books that have been meaningful to Dear One. She has rejected much of the common knowledge associated with allopathic medicine, conventional religion, and mainstream society in general and has replaced it with her own unique world view. These book suggestions represent a pastiche of concepts and images that she likes to think of as the Truth. We are approving the inclusion of this list of suggestions for further reading because they all contain at least some Truth. It's up to you, Dear Reader, to use your intuition to determine which parts are potentially useful to you and which are not.

We have come along at the perfect time in Joy's development to help her affirm a more loving sense of self and encourage a more self-empowered approach to life. We hope that these conversations have had a similar effect on you.

And lastly, but certainly not least-ly, we would encourage each of you to invoke your own personal and dedicated discarnate energies who are sitting on your living room couch right now, waiting patiently for you to recognize them and engage them in conversation. Go ahead. Ask them anything. They have much to tell you that will be helpful and will aid you in living a happier and more fulfilled life.

Final Word from Joy

In the interim between finishing the manuscript and readying the book for publication, I have continued my exploration of topics such as consciousness, the intersection of science and spirituality, and healing, always with an eye out for discrepancies between the ideas being presented and what Pliny has put forth. Happily, I rarely, if ever, find any. Almost everything I think is worth reading or listening to confirms the spirit, if not the letter, of what he has said.

Recently, however, I learned about trauma-informed psychotherapy, and it in no way contradicts what Pliny says, in fact, it adds a new and helpful perspective on the material contained in this book.

Reading and listening to podcasts on the subject, I began to see my life through a lens of trauma. I began remembering all the scary things that happened to me as a child: the emotionally unavailable mother, the distant father, and, oh yes, the haunted house. When I began to consider my ACES (Adverse Childhood Experiences Score), things suddenly made more sense.

Recently, I've begun seeing a trauma-informed sensorimotor psychotherapist and am making great progress doing what she calls "unblending" my traumatized parts.

I want to emphasize that this trauma-based perspective is not inconsistent with what Pliny has said, and I mention it only because of what I see as its tremendous healing value. Besides, Pliny reminds me that if we can help one other person by talking about our experiences, it will make us deliriously happy.

Joy's Suggestions for Further Information

A Course in Miracles, Combined Volume, 3d edition. Edited by Helen Schucman, Bill Thetford, Kenneth Wapnick. New York: Viking: The Foundation for Inner Peace, 1976.

Archer, Rick. *Buddha at the Gas Pump.* https://batgap.com, various dates. [Interviews with spiritually-awakening people.]

Dispenza, Joe. Just about anything he's ever written.

Frankl, Viktor. *Man's Search for Meaning.* Boston: Beacon, 1959.

Geeseman, Suzanne. *Wolf's Message.* Self-published, 2014

Gober, Mark. *An End to Upside Down Thinking.* Sherfield on Loddon, UK: Waterside Press, 2018.

Gober, Mark. *An End to Upside Down Living.* Sherfield on Loddon, UK: Waterside Press, 2020.

Grout, Pam. *E-cubed: Nine More Energy Experiments that Prove Manifesting Magic and Miracles Is Your Full-time Gig.* Carlsbad, CA: Hay House, 2014.

Grout, Pam. *E-squared: Nine Do-It-Yourself Energy Experiments That Prove Your Thoughts Create Your Reality.* Carlsbad, CA: Hay House, 2013.

Hicks, Esther. Just about everything she and Abraham have written or recorded.

Jain, Shamini. *Healing Ourselves: Biofield Science and the Future of Health.* Boulder, CO: Sounds True, 2021.

Lipton, Bruce. Everything he's written.

Moody, Raymond. *Life After Life: The Investigation of a Phenomenon–Survival of Bodily Death.* San Francisco, CA: Harper, 1976.

Moorjhani, Anita. Everything she's written or recorded.

Nepo, Mark. *The Book of Awakening: Having the Life You Want by Being Present to the Life you Have.* 20th ed. Newburyport, MA: Red Wheel, 2020.

Newton, Michael. *Journey of Souls: Case Studies of Life Between Lives.* 5th ed. Woodbury, MN: Llewllyn, 1994.

Rediger, Jeffrey. *Cured: Strengthen Your Immune System and Heal Your Life.* New York: Flatiron, 2020.

Tolle, Eckhart. *The Power of Now: A Guide to Spiritual Enlightenment.* San Francisco: New World Library, 2004.

About the Author

To tell the Truth, which we always do, Joy Graham is not really the author of this book. She's more of a collaborator and a co-conversationalist, and a very good one at that. Her energetic anatomy makes her the perfect partner for us, the collective energies known as Pliny the Elder. She is uniquely suited to receive and transcribe our ideas because she is able to disengage her thinking mind to the degree necessary to receive our wisdom.

Of course, because she is human and currently experiencing life through a human lens, her consciousness is limited. But it is sufficiently porous and flexible enough for us to get our main points across. We are enormously and eternally grateful to her for her diligence, her courage, and her dedication to disseminating our message which will provide comfort and hope to humans dealing with illness of any kind. And that's a lot of humans.

But let us say a few words about the human that is Joy, whom we call Dear One. As a child, she could sense subtle energies, and thus was a perfect target for the discarnates that inhabited her home. She identified them as witches, and they terrified her with their paranormal performances. She told no one of these mostly nocturnal hauntings and as she grew into adolescence, they gradually ceased. But these early experiences left an imprint on her psyche and resulted in an absolute certainty that there is more to life than just the physical.

And to that we can only say, planting a cosmic kiss on her adorable cheek, "Right again, Dear One!"

For more great books from Empower Press
Visit Books.GracePointPublishing.com

EMP⊙WER
P   R   E   S   S

If you enjoyed reading *Pliny Says,* and purchased it through an online retailer, please return to the site and write a review to help others find the book.

www.ingramcontent.com/pod-product-compliance
Lightning Source LLC
Chambersburg PA
CBHW021401090426
42742CB00009B/954